Living Tradition
A Changing Life in Solomon Islands

As told by Michael Kwa'ioloa to Ben Burt

Published for the Trustees of the British Museum
by British Museum Press

First published in 1997 by British Museum Press
A division of The British Museum Company Ltd
46 Bloomsbury Street, London WC1B 3QQ

A catalogue record for this book is available from the British Library

ISBN 0 7141 2533 4

Design, maps and photographs by Ben Burt, unless otherwise stated
Printed in Great Britain by Biddles Ltd, Guildford and Kings Lynn

Contents

Malaita shell money:
part of a 'ten-string'
(*tafuli'ae*), a fathom
long. (half-size)

Acknowledgements

A number of people and organisations have assisted us in writing this book. First of all, Michael Kwa'ioloa would like to thank his relatives and friends for the support they have given him thoughout the various events mentioned in his story, and especially his wife Bizel Fanenalua. Ben Burt is likewise grateful to Annette Ward for support during the research and writing of the book. We both greatly appreciate David Akin's contributions clarifying the culture of Kwaio and Graham Baines' encouragement at the commencement of the project.

Michael Kwa'ioloa's story was recorded during research approved by the Kwara'ae chiefs and Area Council and the government authorities of Malaita and Solomon Islands, and funded in part by the the Nuffield Foundation. In preparing the book we would like to thank Sue Vacarey for typing the draft manuscript, Harry Persaud for providing word-processing facilities, Pauline Khng and Molly Davis for proof-reading, and Carolyn Jones for editing. The costs of publishing the book have been met by the British Museum and we the authors will not receive any payments or royalties from it.

We dedicate this book to Michael Kwa'ioloa's son Ben Burtte'e and all his brothers and sisters of the new generation of Kwara'ae.

Ben Burt and Michael Kwa'ioloa

vi

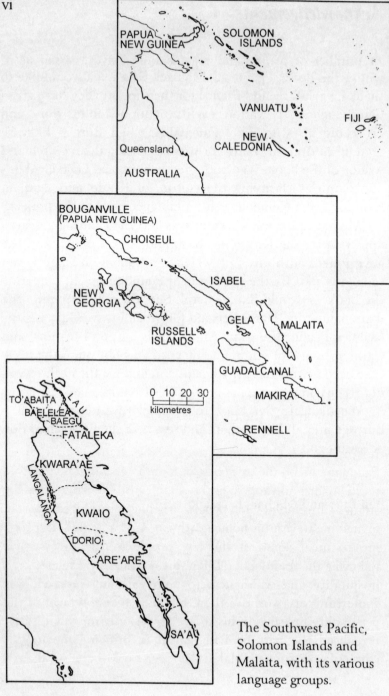

The Southwest Pacific, Solomon Islands and Malaita, with its various language groups.

Introduction

Ben Burt, British Museum, London

My friend Michael Kwa'ioloa grew up in the forested homeland of his ancestors on the Pacific island of Malaita and discovered the wider world by moving to the town of Honiara, capital of Solomon Islands. *Living Tradition* is the story of how his life changed as he came to terms with a world of contrasting cultures and values. This is a common experience for the Islanders of Melanesia but one they seldom share in writing, and Michael Kwa'ioloa's candid description of his personal development, of challenges and achievements, contradictions and setbacks, is also a record of the life and times of his Kwara'ae people and the relationship between their traditional culture and their Christian religion. The subject will be familiar to Malaitan and maybe other Solomon Islands readers, but others will need an introduction to the people, the places and the times he describes. We can begin by looking at how the two of us came to write this book.

I have known Michael since 1979, when I came upon him resting in the shade of a tree on the main footpath near Faumamanu, on the east coast of Kwara'ae. I had just arrived to do my first anthropological research, still bewildered by the strange surroundings and people. Michael introduced himself, invited me to visit his home nearby at Anobala, and later took me to meet some of the few people in the district still following the traditional religion, his relatives in 'Ere'ere. His hospitality and willingness to help with my research was something of a surprise then, but now seems typical of the personality revealed in his story. It was only much later that I realised the part he had played in bringing me to this particular district of Malaita as Secretary of the local Area

Council which had approved the government permit allowing me to research there.

When I returned to Solomon Islands in 1983, Michael and his family were living at Kobito Two, a Malaitan suburb of Honiara. Again he welcomed me to his home and helped with my research, as well as taking me to the doctor when he found me helpless with malaria in my hotel room. On my third visit in 1987 he worked with me full time for a few weeks, and as we walked around his home district in Malaita once again his constant conversation made me realise how much he had to say about the subject of my research, 'tradition and Christianity'. This became the title of my book on the culture and history of Michael's people, the Kwara'ae of Kwai District in East Malaita (Burt 1994). But that is an anthropological study, one of many books describing life in Melanesia through the eyes of a particular kind of *ara'ikwao* or 'whiteman', as my Kwara'ae friends commonly refer to me. Michael was giving me an insider's view of his society, a personal account shaped by his upbringing and continuing commitment to his community. His talent for telling a story suggested a different kind of book, to which he willingly agreed.

Europeans have been writing about the peoples of Solomon Islands for more than a century but books by Islanders are much rarer, and it may be useful to reflect briefly on some of the differences between the two. Anthropologists have recently begun to acknowledge some serious problems with the way we work in regions like Melanesia (as argued convincingly by the anthropologist James Carrier, 1992), which reflect attitudes shared by other Western authors. We can be accused, among other things, of selecting what we write about to indulge our interest in the exotic, in the features of other people's lives which make them seem most different to our own. We create images of other societies to cast a particular light upon our own society and upon the relationship between the two; a relationship which reflects the legacy of colonialism from which anthropology has developed. In particular we seek out what we assume to be the 'traditional' or 'authentic' aspects of people's lives, which we tend to imagine as 'precolonial', somehow existing outside of history, in another world from our own.

It was the romance of this kind of anthropology which first took me to Malaita, reputedly the most culturally conservative island in Solomon Islands, and introduced me to Michael Kwa'ioloa and his people. I had known of the Solomons since my childhood, from reading the novels and travelogues of Jack London, an American who visited the islands in 1908. London delighted in repeating the colonial slander of his time, that Malaita was a land of vicious and degraded savages, and this bleak racist vision of the non-Western world was still pervasive in the British culture of my youth. Anthropology seemed to remove its taint from my own fascination with exotic ways of life, substituting instead a later generation of colonial and anti-colonial stereotypes, which I went to Malaita to explore through my own field research. Getting to know people like Michael personally has been one way of seeing through some of these anthropological myths and mystifications, and Western readers of his autobiography may also find it a useful antidote to the exoticism which still colours both popular and academic literature on Melanesia. As for Melanesians, they may enjoy the novelty of recognising some of their own experiences in a book about themselves.

Even so, an anthropologist's introduction to Michael Kwa'ioloa's background may be necessary to make sense of his story to those unfamiliar with Kwara'ae, Malaita or Solomon Islands. The story begins in Michael's ancestral home in East Kwara'ae or Kwai District, and one man who knew the history of this district better than most was his own father, Samuel Alasa'a, who gave him his education in Kwara'ae traditional values. A few years before he died in 1987, over a hundred years of age, Alasa'a recorded for his sons several cassettes of clan history, which Michael has shared with me. Alasa'a began with the arrival of their first ancestors in Malaita about thirty generations ago and the traditional culture these ancestors established, explaining how they settled and claimed the lands which their descendants have inherited generation after generation since, and how they sacrificed pigs to the ghosts of these ancestors to ensure their spiritual support and protection. Without knowing the Western reckoning of dates, he went on to tell how the first Europeans arrived to recruit labourers for the plantations of Queensland and Fiji (from the 1870s), how his father's generation returned from plantation work with steel tools and new staple crops such as sweet potatoes, and how a British warship tried to bombard their villages (in 1894) in retaliation for an attack on the labour recruiters.

As a young man, Alasa'a witnessed the arrival of the first Australian missionaries of the South Sea Evangelical Mission (SSEM) who set up a station on the offshore island of Ngongosila (in 1906), and he saw some of his own relatives establish the first Christian villages on the coast (in the 1900s and 1910s). Then, like other men of his generation, he went abroad to work for Europeans on a coconut plantation on another island in the Solomons. There he heard rumours of the Great War being fought on the other side of the world and experienced the power of the British colonial government by surviving a murder trial at its capital of Tulagi. Returning home, Alasa'a also encountered William Bell, the District Officer who imposed this government on Malaita and brought an end to the old ways of inter-clan feuding. He helped to bury some people killed by Bell's police when they finally subdued the warriors of East Kwara'ae (in 1919).

In about 1930 Alasa'a married Michael's mother Arana, daughter of 'Arumae Bakete, a famous warrior of the 'Ere'ere clan. They had several children by the time the Japanese and Americans arrived to fight some crucial campaigns of the Second World War on the neighbouring island of Guadalcanal. Responding to the new possibilities which the American presence seemed to offer, the Kwara'ae people then joined the rest of Malaita during the late 1940s in a popular anti-colonial movement known as Māsing Rul (Maasina Rul elsewhere in the island). Their attempt to create a Malaitan alternative to the colonial government raised a debate over traditional and Christian values which continued to preoccupy the next generation, including Alasa'a's youngest son Michael Kwa'ioloa.

By the time Michael was born in 1953, the British authorities had regained control of Malaita but allowed the island its own elected Council. By now the Kwara'ae people had eighty years' experience as migrant labourers on the fringes of the world capitalist economy and thirty years of British colonial rule. The majority of them had become Christians, having rejected the ghosts of their ancestors as colonial domination undermined the power of the traditional leaders they supported. Most, like Michael's parents, belonged to the fundamentalist SSEM, but others included Anglicans and Seventh Day Adventists. Only a few, including some of Michael's close relatives and in-laws, were still, as Kwara'ae call them, 'heathen', following the traditional religion of their ancestral ghosts.

While Michael was growing up in the forest villages of East Kwara'ae, the colonial order of Solomon Islands was undergoing important reforms. The SSEM was being re-organised under indigenous leadership to become the self-governing South Seas Evangelical Church (SSEC) in 1964. The colonial authorities were promoting elected local government and starting to organise Solomon Islands into a nation state, which eventually received political independence in 1978. Michael and his people contributed to the reforms through the organisations which succeeded the Māsing Rul movement; groups of community leaders or 'chiefs', local Church Associations and local government Councils. Behind all these changes was the driving force of post-War economic expansion. The British were developing the commercial economy of Solomon Islands to supply raw materials for growing world markets, and they were building a new administrative and commercial capital at the wartime base of Honiara on Guadalcanal. Kwara'ae men continued to seek their share of the country's growing wealth as migrant labourers, earning cash to supplement the farming way of life which supported them at home. But during the 1960s and '70s more and more of them, like Michael and his family, moved into more specialised occupations in Honiara, where he has spent much of his adult life.

As Michael describes, he has been guided on his way through this changing world both by the traditional culture inherited from his ancestors and by the Christian culture introduced by the Europeans. For Michael and other Kwara'ae, these both represent powerful moral and spiritual forces with often contradictory influences on their lives. As his candid account reveals, many Kwara'ae experience the contrasting values of a tribal society and the ubiquitous Western culture of global capitalism as part of a personal spiritual struggle to resolve contradictions between Christianity and local 'tradition', *falafala*, which Kwara'ae usually translate as 'custom' (Pijin *kastom*) or sometimes as 'culture'. It is this internal struggle which has given Michael the comparative, even relativistic, perspective which enables him to communicate so well to readers familiar only with the Western dimension of his multicultural world.

For Western readers, Michael's story may hold a series of surprises and unexpected insights as it alternately confirms and contradicts their preconceptions about the Pacific Islands. They will probably expect to find his upbringing exotic, as he describes life in villages and gardens in the tropical forests of Malaita, apparently much as his ancestors had experienced it for centuries. In fact Michael himself could tell them how much it had changed since his father's childhood. In going to school and enjoying a wild youth in town, Michael may seem to be entering the more familiar and mundane world of Western culture. But how Western is his experience of town life when it comes to depend upon the spiritual power of ancestral ghosts? And if his subsequent conversion to born-again Christianity seems to bring him back into the Western world, how typical of the West is a Christianity of visions and miracles which pervades his whole life with spiritual power? Then again, how Christian is Kwara'ae society when it constantly threatens to relapse into traditional practices such as blood feuding, restitution payments and bridewealth gifts, which many Kwara'ae themselves regard as 'heathen'?

In trying to live the traditional culture his father taught him, Michael has also tried to bridge the divisions which these contradictions have created in Kwara'ae society. Even as a Christian, he is at home among his relatives in the few Kwara'ae families still worshipping the ghosts of their ancestors, segregated from Christian society by the incompatibility of traditional and Christian religious rules. It is his own experience of their way of life, the epitome of 'tradition' among a tradition-conscious people, which enables him to appreciate the power of the ancestral religion which he and his family have rejected.

If Michael's religious world-view holds surprises for Westerners, his involvement in the developing capitalist economy of Solomon Islands may also be more than it seems.

Even when most immersed in a money-earning business as a building contractor in Honiara, it soon becomes clear that his dreams of Western wealth owe as much to Melanesian ideals of leadership and prestige through mutual help and gift-exchange as to capitalist values of material accumulation and consumerism. In his satisfaction at giving employment to his clan brothers, as in his voluntary work as Secretary and spokesman for the Kwara'ae chiefs, Michael's ambitions focus not only on making a living for his large family but also on playing an important and useful role in his Kwara'ae community. Even in Honiara his life is still deeply rooted in the land and tradition of his ancestors in Malaita, while he seeks the benefits of economic development abroad.

People in this position are often described as living in 'two worlds', but although Westerners might like to see it in these terms, the Kwara'ae seem to treat their experience of town and rural life, of Western and local culture, as contrasting aspects of a single world, inextricably linked. Men from Malaita have been coming to town for more than 120 years now, since their ancestors began working in Fiji and Queensland. For most of them, Malaita is still 'home' (*fanoa*), even in the longstanding communities which have transplanted Malaitan life to the suburbs around Honiara, and their homeland remains a source of economic, social and cultural security to them. However, this has not prevented inevitable tensions between life at home and abroad, between tradition and the Western culture of global capitalism.

Michael's story demonstrates the glamour of this culture, which goes far beyond the Christianity, medicine and education valued by his father's generation. The Western-style 'development' which so enthuses many Kwara'ae today also entails the beer-drinking, the casual mixing of men and women, the rock music and the fancy clothes which interested Michael as a young man, as well as the modern amenities and the cash to pay for them which still keep him and his family in Honiara. Even so, Michael continues to proclaim the values of the self-sufficient rural economy and the local control of political and cultural development which his people have struggled so hard to maintain, symbolised by the image of 'tradition' which he so often invokes. It may be easier for others to see the contradictions in these positions than for those who have to make choices between them for their own lives and communities. If Michael's opinions sometimes seem to shift between the conflicting values symbolised by 'tradition' and 'development' as well as 'Christianity' and 'backsliding', this is a useful reminder of how difficult it can be to deal with the pressures of life in a society changing as rapidly as Kwara'ae in the second half of the 20th century.

Of course the notion of tradition has itself become a way of coming to terms with these changes, as a growing anthropological literature explores (see Keesing & Tonkinson 1982, Jolly & Thomas 1992). While anthropologists have come to recognise that tradition can change and develop, people like the Kwara'ae often find that images of antiquity and permanence lend certainty and authenticity to their own efforts to control the values tradition represents. But only those whose conception of tradition is stuck in the precolonial past of anthropological or Kwara'ae myth would regard Michael's experiences as non-traditional or inauthentic. His own respect for the tradition of his father and ancestors reveals a more realistic attitude with equally strong roots in Kwara'ae culture. For the Kwara'ae, tradition originates in the past but serves the present and future, finding itself reaffirmed as well as challenged by Christianity and Western culture. Focussing on the tradition of their ancestors helps people shape for themselves the Christian culture they wish to live by, but life has never been so simple that they could expect to devise a cultural tradition without contradictions, and particularly in times of rapid social change.

One ancient and traditional contradiction in Kwara'ae culture in particular is illustrated in Michael's story, in his relationship with his wife and in the glimpses he gives of the role of women under the traditional religion. In the past women's reproductive powers were treated as defiling and damaging to the ancestral ghosts and to the men who mediated their spiritual power. As Kwara'ae men are fond of saying, in Malaita the man is in charge, among Christians as among those worshipping the ghosts. Michael's wife Bizel Fanenalua, the kind-hearted, patient and hard-working mother of their ten children, will have her own view of some of the incidents in her husband's story, in which she has played an important part. But she does not have a voice of her own here, and as a modest, rather shy person, her version of events would be impossible for a 'whiteman' like myself to record. Fanenalua's account will have to be left to the readers' imagination, as an example of the contradiction between men's and women's interests which Kwara'ae share with all other cultural traditions. Even so, they should bear in mind that, despite the domestic problems and disputes which Michael recounts, she has continued to support him through some difficult times. Between them they ran the happiest and best organised family of twelve people that I could ever imagine crammed into a little three-room house, still finding space to welcome guests, including a stream of relatives from Malaita and myself.

Finally, we can return to consider Michael's authorship of this book and his purpose in having his story published. The book follows several other autobiographies from Melanesia, some written with the help of anthropologists (as the following references indicate). Those from Malaita range from the old-fashioned big-man 'Elota of Kwaio, who made his mark in a still largely autonomous local community (Keesing 1978), through Jonathan Fifi'i, who confronted the colonial authorities as a leader of the Māsing Rul movement (Fifi'i and Keesing 1989), to Sir Frederick Osifelo, who made his way up through the colonial administration to become the first Speaker of the Solomon Islands Legislative Assembly (Osifelo 1985). Like other Melanesian autobiographers, including Gideon Zoleveke of Choiseul in Western Solomons (Zoleveke 1980), Ongka the Highlands Papua New Guinea big-man (Strathern 1979), and Somare, the Prime Minister of Papua New Guinea (Somare 1975), these men were political leaders for changing times. Their stories are sources for the Pacific histories now being written, and they help to explain how Melanesians themselves see the new societies they have created under colonial domination.

Although Michael has played a full and active part in the affairs of his local community, as pastor and preacher, Secretary to the Kwara'ae Area Council and to the Kwara'ae chiefs, he would not claim to be one of the 'important men' (*ngwae 'inoto 'a*) of his people. What he does have, which such big-men often lack, is a talent for communicating what it feels like to live through the common experiences of his particular time and place. Because of the unprecedented changes overtaking Kwara'ae society and tradition, Michael believes his experience has something to offer others. As he explains it,

I was born of the father of chiefs, and I don't want to hide all the things he told me. I want to educate other Kwara'ae families so they'll understand the old way of life my father passed on to me, to educate present and future generations in the things which not only my own father but other chiefs also taught me, to show how life has changed. Otherwise it might be lost. If something happened to me, my children wouldn't know about the changes during my lifetime, so I want it documented, written down for them to read. It is important to trace my life back to the things which are no more, which I no longer see.

This is what I have helped him to do, as an anthropologist and friend. But the critiques of Melanesian anthropology mentioned above extend to the way we edit and interpret other people's autobiographies into a Western form of narrative (see Keesing and Jolly 1992:229), so I feel my role should be acknowledged and explained, rather than obscured or denied.

Michael and I recorded his autobiography on cassette in 1987, with additions in 1991 and 1993. Michael spoke in Solomons Pijin, the language in which we are both fluent but which, despite its English-derived vocabulary, has developed to express Melanesian concepts rather than European ones. I acted as interviewer, prompting accounts of whatever might be interesting and explanations of whatever might seem obscure to an audience less familiar with Kwara'ae culture. Our work together had already made Michael adept in explaining Kwara'ae culture to me, representing the foreigners to whom he is also speaking in this book. I have edited his narrative and put it into chronological order where necessary, and in beginning at the beginning, so to say, I have followed his inclinations as well as my own. Then I have translated his words into English fairly loosely, cutting many of the repetitive and redundant phrases which occur in an oral account but trying to keep the tone of the original narrative, so characteristic of Michael's personality. In doing this, I have had to add no more than three or four linking phrases throughout the whole text. Michael himself made a number of small amendments and added a few new sentences when he checked and approved the edited manuscript, and I also included a paragraph from one of his letters.

In order for the book to read fluently as an English language text I have avoided using Kwara'ae words unless it seemed impossible to translate them. Where translations and other points require clarification, I have explained them in footnotes, which mostly reflect my own interpretations of Michael's narrative. Lastly, I have chosen and captioned the illustrations, which are all from my own photographs, except where stated otherwise.

Most of my editorial work on Michael's story was done in the relaxing atmosphere of certain London pubs, where I allowed his words to evoke my own memories of the time I have spent in Solomon Islands. No doubt this has also left its trace on the way I have presented his story, for recording it has also been part of a formative personal experience of my own. But although this book is a collaborative effort between Michael Kwa'ioloa and myself, we agree that it reflects Michael's own view of his experience, as far as a book in the English language can. We have tried to produce a story which readers in Kwara'ae, Solomon Islands and beyond will enjoy while they learn something both new and traditional about changing life in the contemporary Pacific.

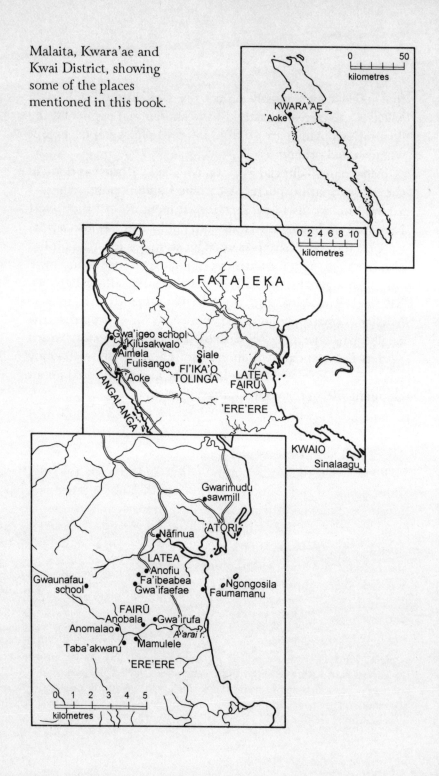

Malaita, Kwara'ae and Kwai District, showing some of the places mentioned in this book.

1 *Early Years*

I want to tell the story of my life, from the time I was a small boy until the present. I was born in 1953 at a place called Gwa'ifaefae in Kwai District in Malaita. My name is Michael Kwa'ioloa and my father was Samuel Alasa'a. We come from Siale but our land and all our belongings are at Tolinga, and we moved down from our original homes and found the places at Fairū where we live now.[1] My father taught me everything, because he was a traditional chief and the father of chiefs, who lived more than a hundred years. He saw his grandfathers and fathers kill people and he knew who they killed. He held a piece of a man they'd killed, he saw how they baked it and maybe he was frightened to eat it, but he probably tasted it. My father was afraid to tell me, but he must have tasted it because how would he know that human meat is so cold you have to put it in the fire before you can put it in your mouth? If you take it out for a couple of minutes it's too cold to eat. If you haven't eaten it you can't talk like that. I believe he tasted man, and he was the father of chiefs.

I'll say what I know about my father and what he told me about some of the things he did. My father was a priest for the ghosts, but when the mission gained strength and everyone came into the church he too left his pagan ways and came to church. As a priest my father cooked pigs for the ghosts as sacrifices for the lives of our families and relatives. If someone was sick and a ghost asked for a pig by coming to possess my father, then he'd tell the man whose child was sick to catch a

---

1 Siale is an ancient shrine, widely regarded as the original settlement of the ancestors of Kwara'ae about thirty generations ago. Tolinga is nearby and its people were one of several clans which continued to belong to the Siale shrine. They began to move down to Fairū near the coast from about six generations ago.

pig and he'd carry it away to offer as a sacrifice to the ghost. Then the ghost would cure the sickness and the child would be healed.

My father did this for some time, but what made him come to the church was his children. Ten of us were born, but five died and only five lived. He kept on sacrificing pigs and my brothers and sisters kept on dying. Every time one died he tried again, and although Satan's power was strong,[2] perhaps somehow my father wasn't doing things properly or our families and relatives weren't looking after the ghosts well or something like that. So the ghosts made trouble for us and the children just died. Some may have died of malaria, I don't know, because in the past we didn't know about these things. This was long ago, before I was born, but my father told me that he came down to the church because my five brothers and sisters died. He tried as hard as he could to avoid the other five of us dying too, so that was the reason father and mother said 'Maybe we ought to change our ways and go down to join the church to worship God.'

My father told me this because I asked him 'Why did the other five die? I should have had more brothers and sisters so there'd be lots of us living happily together.' But my father said 'They died because that's how the ghosts are, and we didn't have clinics or hospitals in the past where we could easily go for treatment.' That's what my father told me. Sometimes we'd struggle to make local medicine, scraping tree bark or cutting leaves or taking roots, cutting and grating them, heating them up and squeezing them out, to put on

2   The Kwara'ae follow European missionaries in identifying the ghosts (*akalo*) of their ancestors with Satan, calling them 'devils' (*defolo* or *devol*), and those who worship them 'heathen' (*hitini* or *hiden*) in English (and Pijin). But this does not mean they regard the ghosts or their religion as evil, as the missionaries do, which is why 'ghosts' and 'pagans' are used here as more appropriate translations for the Pijin words used by Kwa'ioloa.

sores or to drink, but that didn't work either. That's why it was hard for my brothers and sisters to survive and they died. One of them, Alasa'a, injured himself by burning his leg and he died from a big sore. Today, even if he'd cut his leg off, I've seen people in hospital with legs cut off who are still alive. But at that time people could even die from small sores. Looking back to when I was small makes me think how lucky we are today. In the past things were hard; no medicines, no doctors or anything.

That was the life which made my father come down and join the others in the church. He said he'd stay with the church and be faithful to its work and when they saw that he was, they got him to help in the church, to pray and look after church activities and the kitchen utensils like plates, pots, cups and spoons, as a deacon in the church. Before that he'd been living in 'Ere'ere, while he was a priest. When he came into the church he moved down to Gwa'ifaefae and that's what I remember when I was small. Maybe there was somewhere else before Gwa'ifaefae, but all I know is that when I was small and my father took me into the church during services it was at Gwa'ifaefae, just above Anofiu. The pastor there was Timi John, and Enoch Manibili was a pastor too, when I was small. They were brothers of my father, from our own clan and born from brothers, so they were my fathers.[3] They were pagans before too, but they'd accepted Jesus and when they were experienced enough to look after the church as pastors they organised all the people into one village and built the church. I was small and still didn't understand everything, but I know it was at Gwa'ifaefae that my father worked for the church.

3 In ordinary conversation Kwara'ae often do not distinguish between real fathers and fathers' brothers, real brothers and the sons of fathers' brothers, real mothers and mothers' sisters, and so on. As we shall see, Kwa'ioloa's story includes many fathers and brothers beyond his immediate family.

I can still remember when I was a small child being with my mother, and her name was Arana. She was a woman from 'Ere'ere. My father married her and she bore the five of us children. Our firstborn is John Maesatana. The second was Filistus Sango'iburi, who's now dead. The third is Authaban Maniramo, then there's myself, and then the last one's called Arana junior, a girl. She was named after my mother, but first she was called Maefunua and when mother died they changed it.

When I was very small all I did was suck milk from my mother's breast. I know my mother cared for me well, and when I was small all I did was play with the children of the village and I didn't do anything else until I got hungry, and then I came back and called for food. I didn't wear any clothes; I was naked. I remember we slept on leaf mats, me and my mother, because although we could buy other mats mother didn't like sleeping on them. She said they were slippery and she preferred a local leaf mat. We usually slept close to the fire. We'd put down a piece of tree bark and put the leaf mat on top to sleep on. I can still remember when I was a child of about three years old, walking about and playing around, but still naked. With my mother caring for me, even if I wanted to go to the toilet in the middle of the night, she'd take a leaf, put it down, I'd do it on the leaf and she'd just take it to the toilet. That's how well my mother looked after me.

While we lived at Gwa'ifaefae when I was small, I remember all our houses in those days had no floors. The houses were just built with bamboo walls but they were low and the doorways were small too. We didn't use hardboard and things for making doors like today, just tree bark to close the doorway. The roofs were sago-palm leaf and poles. There were no nails either and they just used lawyer cane for rope, but they really knew how to lash with it and it could last for ten or fifteen years on a house. I practised doing it when I lived at home and my father often showed me how to tie it, but now I find it a bit confusing and maybe I'd have to trace it out on paper. I missed some of that training, but it's a very good training to get.

At that time there were no kitchens with our houses either, because the cooking was done inside the same house. There was a big fire with a platform up above for putting the firewood on and for keeping traditional shell money in bundles where the smoke could rise and preserve it. The leaf mat would get dirty but inside it would be as good as ever and the red colour would stay bright because of the heat and the string of the shell money wouldn't weaken or go rotten.[4] Even if it stayed there for years and years, when it was taken out it was still just as good. The house didn't have rooms inside. The front part where you went in was the place where they cooked the food and on the opposite side to the hearth was a bench for putting food on, sweet potatoes and yams. The firewood was on a rack above the fire so that the fire would warm it and make it burn well. Then next to it was another fire with a rack above it too, but that was where my mother put all the leaf mats, and on that one they also put a rack made of split bamboo as a platform for putting nuts on, to warm them over the fire. They'd be smoked so the kernels would dry out and when we cracked them we'd make them into a special pudding, very good to eat and very oily, made with taro.[5]

4 'Shell money' (*mani*) is strings of shell beads, the most valuable being of red shell, which are strung in standard denominations and used for important ceremonial presentations and exchanges.

5 Ngali-nuts (canarium almonds) are an important seasonal harvest and taro is a Melanesian staple root-crop. Pudding is made by pounding such foods in a wooden bowl.

The back part of the house was a big platform which took up the whole of the floorspace and on it were our beds for sleeping, all in a row. There was a wall down the middle of the platform dividing the girls' sleeping place from the boys'. This was just our brothers and sisters, no-one else. Mother would sleep with the girls on one side and father would sleep with us boys on the other side. Otherwise the area was open, but when we went to sleep no-one else could go there. During the night it was tabu for anyone to come in.

If a visitor came he couldn't sleep in the house. There was a big men's house which everyone co-operated to build, so he could go there to sleep, with the older boys. All the boys of the village would sleep in the one house, because there was no selfishness in those days. Nowadays if a man builds his own house his children sleep with him, and if a visitor comes and there's no house of that kind he just has to go away again. Women who came to visit would sleep with the other women, but the man of the house would go to sleep in the men's house if all the women visitors were in his house. There was another part of the men's house for the old men and one man of the village had to stay there with the young men. He'd stay there to keep the fire burning, but the young men - you know young men like to live well - they'd make a floor so they could be more comfortable.[6]

When I was a small child I really just relied on my mother for everything, so if I wasn't with her I felt sad and unhappy. While I played I watched the path for her to come back, but most of the time I just cried to go to the garden. I remember going to the garden and watching my mother do all kinds of garden work, and being amazed by what I saw. I'd wait there all day until I was tired. Sometimes I'd cry to go home, but

6 In old-fashioned earth-floored houses, people would sleep near the fire to keep warm at night, but more modern houses have raised slat floors.

mother couldn't take me back because she really enjoyed doing the garden work. When I went to the garden, until I was about seven, they didn't teach me and I'd just watch, because I wasn't able to work. They'd say 'You have to watch how people work', but I'd just play and even though I sometimes pretended to work, I wasn't able to.

When we arrived at the garden in the morning, mother would pray and when she'd finished she'd tell me to go and sit in the shade. She'd put me in a place which was shady and cool and that's where she'd leave her leaf mats and cords for carrying the bundles back to the house in the evening. She'd take out the bushknife and axe and father and her would go ahead with the work in the forest. When I was small it amazed me to watch as they cut down the forest, cleared the ground, sometimes making fires and throwing on the trees they'd cut for the fire to burn them. Then when they'd cleared away the forest they'd bring taro stems and plant them in the ground to make a garden. We used to have big gardens. I often watched as they weeded the taro, when it was growing well, looking good, growing big and forming tubers.

They'd lay out the taro garden in plots, not in one wide area. In Kwara'ae there are several reasons for making these plots. Sometimes they'd make a plot to a value of shell money and if a man were to buy it he'd have to give one red money to take the crop to eat.[7] And plots meant the garden was ready in stages. When the first part of the garden was ripe and ready to harvest we ate the crop up to there, but after that the next part of the garden would grow up. Besides, laying the garden out in plots reflected our way of life. People would come by the gardens along the path and look along the plots we'd laid out and how we'd lined up the poles marking them

---

7 'Red money' is a general term for the largest denominations of shell money, which include the more valuable red beads.

out and say 'Eh, this man really knows how to make a garden! Look how he's lined up the tree trunks he's cut to make it look nice.' That's the way we were.

In those days there was plenty of taro. I remember when my mother had pulled up the taro she'd just poke the soil with the point of her bushknife and stick one or two sweet potato vines into the ground. She wasn't really planting them, but when they spread over the ground the soil was full of potatoes. In those days food was far better than today. That's why my mother and father didn't make sweet potato gardens, just taro. Mother would stick a few potatoes in the ground, but most of our people wouldn't eat potatoes, and the adults would just eat taro.[8] But you don't see this nowadays, and when I compare the gardening I don't see us working like that. Every day we'd go to the garden to produce food, and that's how we were. Now we come to Honiara and earn money, but we don't eat well because when we go to the market to buy food it's so limited. There isn't the freedom to take as much as you can carry, and that's hard.

In the daily gardening routine my father and mother followed, they'd go on till about three o'clock and then my father would tell my mother 'Go and pull up the taros, clean them, bundle them and carry them home, so you can be home first to make the evening meal.' In those days leaf mats were used as bags.[9] They'd lay out a leaf mat, put another mat at the top, another mat across, and arrange the taro on it. The cords were laid underneath and when it was full they'd put another mat around it and tie it up with the taro inside. Then

8 Sweet potatoes were introduced to Malaita in the 19th century and, although now the main staple, are regarded as inferior to traditional foods like taro.

9 These mats, also used as rain capes (hence called 'umbrellas' in English), are made of strips of pandanus leaf sewn together to form a flat sack.

besides this I'd see my mother put some more taro into yet another leaf mat to put on top of this big bundle she was carrying back to the house. She kept that one in case she met some of her in-laws or brothers or sisters or other relatives along the path, because it would be very embarrassing to carry this big load of food and just pass by any of our relatives on the way home. This was really important, because we'd often meet brothers and sisters and as I followed behind I'd see them meet. They'd say 'Oh hello. On your way back from the garden?' 'Yes.' Then she'd talk for a while and say, 'Eh, take a little taro to cook when you get home and have a bit to eat'. Even if the person said 'That's all right,' no, she'd give it to him; 'If you don't want it, just throw it away somewhere.' She'd force him to take the taro, because that's the way some of us were, very kind to other people. It was our tradition to share our food with others.

On our way, when we were nearly home, there was a stream of water, the Ba'ufa stream at Anofiu halfway along the path. So mother would come by and fill up her bamboo bottles, bundle them together and carry something like five or ten of them. And that was with the big load too, on top of the taro. What's more, as she went along, despite the size of the load, without putting it down she'd go to the side of the path and pull some leaves for the stone oven.[10] She'd take them in her hand, bundle them up and add them to the top of the load. And sometimes, going along, she'd see greens at the side of the path, wild ones such as ferns and sandpaper cabbage[11] and she'd go with that big load, pick them, bundle them up and take them to the house too. It really amazed me when I

10 For an oven, stones are heated on the fire and the food is steamed on them, wrapped and covered in leaves from plants such as gingers or banana.

11 Edible wild greens or 'cabbage' (Pijin *kabis*, Kwara'ae *tatabu*) include various ferns and leaves. 'Sandpaper cabbage' (*'amau*) is a small fig tree.

was small, but for my mother it was her normal work and she never got tired. Maybe she was tired, but I didn't know, because every day was the same. She never changed or said 'Oh, I was so tired yesterday, I'm not going today.' No; when morning came she'd say she had to go. And my father was a man for working in the garden too and I thought he'd be tired, but he wasn't. Except on market days, when they both went to market to get fish for us.

Then when we reached the house in the afternoon I'd play but mother would be working hard, unpacking the taro and everything, preparing the meal, making the stone oven, taking the saucepans and mugs and things and running to the stream, bathing and washing everything and coming back to the house. Back at the house she'd make a stew with the greens, when the oven was done; a nice stew with tomatoes and anything you could buy at the market. When we'd prepared food for the meal for about five o'clock, I'd see father coming. From the time we reached the house I'd be watching for father and when he arrived I'd run to meet him as he came into the village, saying 'Father's coming, father's coming.' Then when mother had finished cooking and everything was done she'd say 'Let's eat'. They'd uncover that nice oven of taro, so good to eat, and they'd serve the stew, sometimes in a coconut shell. Although there were plates, they preferred to eat from coconut because they said it was cooler and nicer to eat from.

When we'd finished eating the wooden gong would call out. We usually ate early so that when the gong called we could go to evening worship. When we came out from worship it was still not quite dark and we'd reach the house and be sitting for a while by the time it got dark. After dark I often saw my parents and the parents from neighbouring houses meet together. They'd carry the small children and we'd gather in an open space and put down leaf mats and the pieces of tree bark we used for lying down on by the fire or anything else we could find, and we'd sit down and talk. We children would chat and play around and the adults would talk until it was time for the children to go to sleep. That was when our fathers would discuss their plans; tomorrow's work, what we'd do at the weekend, cleaning up the village area on the Friday, when to go fishing or hunting or gathering nuts, and things like that.

While my father was in the church they chose him as village chief, and I know a little about that too. I wasn't very big, but I remember that many evenings my father would beat the gong and everyone would gather, bringing tree bark or bits of wood, and sitting down in the leaf-shelter.[12] Then my father would speak to them. He'd talk about tradition and how to maintain a good way of life. Things like 'I forbid lots of women to go and fill up their bamboo bottles at the same waterspout and talk about someone. One of them is going to say "That woman said so and so about you" to one of the others. I forbid it, because it's all right talking like that but when that woman gets back she'll tell someone else, and when it reaches the man you were talking about he's going to react, and there might be bloodshed. Or someone may have to give him some shell money,[13] or a fight could break out.' That's what I used to hear my father tell them. I do the same when I instruct my children and my wife and my sisters. He'd say 'You keep your mouths shut, and if you hear anybody say something about someone and say "Go and tell him", you say "No, go and tell him yourself. It's none of my business and if I tell him, my husband's going to beat me, because the kind of thing you're talking about leads to trouble."' So my father

12 Villages often have an open-sided leaf-thatched shelter (*gwaurau*) used for feasts and public gatherings.

13 Shell money may be demanded as restitution (*fa 'aā bu 'a*) for an offence or as compensation (*du 'unga 'a*) for an injury.

would say 'Don't do it'. He'd also tell people to attend church services faithfully and teach their children well, he'd arrange work parties to clear the village area and the paths to the drinking and bathing streams and the toilets, and he'd ask them to fence their pigs to avoid them causing damage.

I remember all the things my father taught me, because he'd often teach us in the evenings too. He'd have a good look round, close the door, we'd sit down and he'd teach us. I asked him, 'Father, why do you close the door when we sit down, before you teach us?' Then he said 'That's tradition. If I teach you all while one or two boys from other families are with us and you disobey, they'll take all the good advice and benefit their families when they grow up, and you'll be out of luck. That's why I have to teach you all alone inside our house, so even if you're not capable of learning from it, it will only fall on the ground.' The teaching he gave us was to obey the two of them, mother and him, and when they told us something we had to do it. When they were both there we'd pray, they'd shut the door, teach us, and we'd talk. He'd say 'Don't strike another man's child, because if you hit a child and beat him up and he dies, you'll be in trouble too. We'll have to pay compensation and things like that. Children can die, so don't beat another man's child, or throw a stone at him. When you're angry, don't say hard things.' That's what it was like, because my father was a village chief and it was he who spoke for us all. He went on to teach us that we mustn't take anything belonging to someone else without permission, because if we do that it's stealing. Even if we find a chicken has laid an egg, we don't take an egg belonging to someone else. He taught us that if we went past someone's garden and saw some good maize or sugar cane, we mustn't take it. We mustn't throw things at people's pigs, or at people's chickens. We mustn't go off with other children in case they got bitten by a poisonous snake or fell from a tree or drowned in a

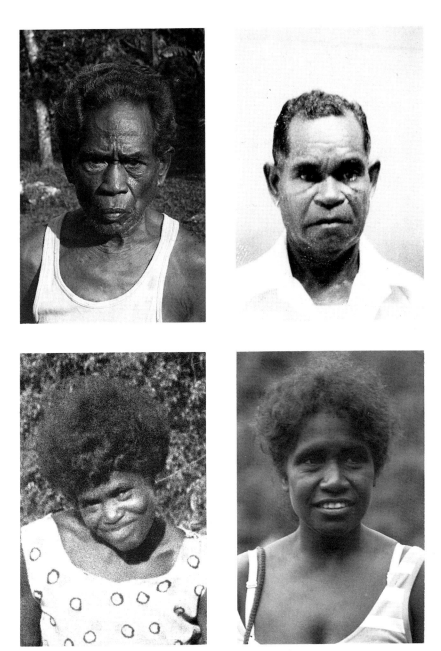

Some of Kwa'ioloa's family: his father Samuel Alasa'a (1979),
his eldest brother John Maesatana (from a 1980s passport photo),
his elder sister Filistus Sango'iburi (1979), and his younger sister Ivery Arana
(1993).

Gardening: a husband and wife work together to extend their garden of taro, growing in the foreground. (1979)

Preparing a meal: a woman peels taro with a pearlshell knife, in a house like that of Kwa'ioloa's childhood, with the private sleeping room at the back. (1979)

A forest village of thatched houses, planted with decorative croton and cordyline shrubs. (1983)

Boys at play in an old-fashioned community in 'Ere'ere. (1979)

The wharf at 'Aoke, provincial capital of Malaita, with the *Compass Rose*, one of the ships travelling between Malaita and Honiara. (1987)

Shops along Mendana Avenue, the main street in the business centre of Honiara. (1991)

stream. Because if we did any of these things, they could take us to court, and we could be fined or go to prison.[14]

Then they went on to teach us that we must care for each other in the house, be kind to each other and share our food with our brothers and sisters, big and small. We mustn't be naughty and spoil things in the house. They taught us not to play with sharp knives in case they cut us, to be careful with everything in the house and not to damage it. And they told us we had to respect the old people and not play around with them or throw things at them or say bad things to them. If I see they need help, I must help them; if they're carrying their belongings and they're heavy, I must carry some of them and accompany them to the house. That's what they told me. Their teaching covered so many subjects. And they told me I must be willing to work, because if I wasn't I'd come to no good and when I married I wouldn't have a good house and I wouldn't have a good job or a good garden or anything else. Because a lazy man doesn't achieve anything. And besides, if a man's lazy and doesn't do well for himself, people will talk about him and his family and he'll get a bad reputation, because a lazy family steals from other people's gardens.

When my father was looking after me he'd stop me from holding razor blades or sharp knives, but my mother would get cross because I'd cry for the knife I'd been holding. My mother Arana would say 'Just leave him; let him hold it until he starts playing and puts it down and then you can hide it'. But my father would say 'No, he mustn't hold it. You're giving him too much freedom. He mustn't hold it in case he injures himself. If he falls on it or cuts himself we'll have all the trouble of taking him to hospital. He'll waste money and waste time and you'll blame yourself.'

14   This last warning is because people are held responsible for the wellbeing of their companions, even if they come to harm by accident.

When I'm a bit hasty in beating my own children, I think of how my father was when I was small. When the two of us went to the garden he'd carry me as well as taking his axe and carrying wood for the fire. When we got halfway along the path he'd be really tired and he'd put me down and say 'Okay Michael, now you can walk'. When he did that and he'd walked a few steps, you'd expect me to move too, but no, I wouldn't move a foot. I'd just sit down on the ground and cry. Then my father would speak more sternly; 'Michael, come along quickly!' He'd talk until he was angry and I began to be frightened, but I could see in his eyes that he was sorry for me and he'd say 'Run along quickly and I'll carry you again'. I was the ruin of my father. But when they disciplined me they really taught me to be willing to work, and that's something I appreciate as an adult. As I work I know my mother did the right thing, and it's made me teach my children the same way. The same things my mother taught me, I've passed on to my own family, and it works.

2 *Life Without Mother*

When I was six years old we moved to a neighbouring village called Anofiu, beside the Faubaba stream. That was my first time to play in the water in a big stream and I really enjoyed life there with the other boys. Then, when I was seven years old, my mother died. By that time they were teaching me to use my hands and work. When they went to the gardens they'd make me work, and when I came back I had to help with work around the house too.

Then as time went on my mother fell sick. When she was sick she no longer felt like following her usual ways and going to the garden every day. That's how it began; this hard working woman, my mother, didn't want to go to the garden. So I asked my father, 'Why are just you and my big sister going to the garden, but my mother watches us go and won't go to the garden herself?' 'Oh, your mother has this feeling in her chest. That's why she's unable to go. Her back hurts, her chest hurts; it's like a pain all over her body.' I know now that what affected her chest must have been something wrong with her lungs. It must have been TB, because of all the hard work, always using fire, being in the sun and carrying heavy loads. Day by day she no longer looked after me and my little sister, the one born after me. When my younger sister was only a few months old, she died.

I remember one afternoon my mother was much worse and my father wouldn't go anywhere. He stayed in the house, and my big sister Sango'iburi didn't go out either. They could see she was in a very bad state and coming near to death, and that's why they were staying quietly at home. Then eventually I remember the gong calling for the church service, and when the gong called my mother got up and her breath left her body. When she sat down I saw her fall over and die. Then my father straightened her out on the bed and they all cried. As they cried over her I wasn't too sad because I wasn't very big and when she died I was just playing. All our relatives came to offer us their sympathy and they stayed for a week, day and night. The day after she died they stayed with her until evening and then they buried her. They buried her at Anofiu, our old village.

When my mother died things were really bad. So many times I wanted to see her again, but I couldn't. But it was good for me to see them bury her, because my father said 'Mother's dead; she's gone into the ground.' The day they buried my mother I could see my father was really sad; so sad. As he carried me and my little sister Arana he just cried with us. When we'd buried my mother and I'd come back I could see my sister Sango'iburi and my brother Maniramo were really sad. They came and sat in the house quietly, not saying anything, just crying. But the other families came and stayed with us during the night, until dawn, during the morning, throughout the day, until the night. They stayed a full week before going home. During that time I felt the loss of my mother. I had no mother now. The women who lived near our house said 'You can treat us as mothers, because your mother was our sister'. But no, I couldn't treat them as mothers. In my heart I knew that we didn't have a mother, just a father. Then I began to love my father more than my mother, and that's how my little sister and me used to treat him. We stayed with him during the night and we had to sleep with him, me on one side, her on the other, and if he wasn't there during the night we had a bad time. We just slept together and were really frightened. At that time my sister Ivery Arana was very small. She must have been about eighteen months, because she used to cry for milk to my father. He was up all night with her and he used to give her to a woman called Maefurifuri, my aunt, and she used to suckle her when she was small.[1]

Then, when I was eight years old, we moved again to a village at Fa'ibeabea, above the village where I was born at Gwa'ifaefae. We lived with another of our fathers, Manilofia, who was born of the same ancestors as my father. We stayed there until I was about twelve. I remember how I spent my time going around in the forest with the other boys, eating nuts, climbing trees, cutting them so they fell down with us in them, climbing up one tree and going along to another tree somewhere else, and then down again. We just spent our time playing. Then my uncle Patrick Nunute'e Aburofau from Gwa'irufa and his wife came and asked my father and two sisters and brother to go over to another place called Anomalao, beside the A'arai river over in Fairū. We moved from Latea to Fairū, our own land, lived at Anomalao for a couple of years and then moved to where our garden was, at Gwa'irufa. That was where I started to grow up.

While we were living at Gwa'irufa I grew bigger and walked around, but I was still naked and I spent my time playing around the village clearing. But my father made a strict rule at that time; during the day I had to go to the garden with my sister. If I didn't go to the garden in the day they'd beat me and they ruled that I couldn't eat that evening. I had to go hungry until morning. And they told the relatives in the other houses not to allow me into the house and not to give me any food. Often when I received this punishment I'd sleep outside the door under the floor of the house. That's how they treated me when I misbehaved. My father would tell me that if I didn't work until evening, played all day and

---

1 In Kwara'ae, fathers' sisters, mothers' brothers and their children are 'aunt' (*'a'ai*), 'uncle' (*ngwai*) and 'cousin' (*di'i*), as distinct from 'mother' (including mother's sisters), 'father' (including father's brothers), 'brother' and so on.

then I ate food, I'd be stealing the food. That wasn't the way to eat and I shouldn't be eating. When they treated me like that, when I'd done nothing all day, I was ashamed and afraid to go near the house. But when I thought about being punished and got frightened I was more willing to help my sister and brother, and when I went to the garden I learnt to work with them, even though I was young. I'd help them cut trees, do the weeding and carry bundles of taro stems when it was time to go home.[2]

But after my mother died I didn't know who to call mother, because I was only little. We no longer had a mother and things were hard. And my father only stayed with us for a short while, because we had no money. It seems our family needed things we didn't have, on the money side. As far as goods were concerned we were all right because we had pigs, we had gardens, we had all the ordinary things we needed day to day. What we didn't have was money. We needed things like cloth and salt and soap and kerosene, and we needed all that very badly. Even apart from those things, we needed to buy axes, saucepans for cooking and things for the house. I didn't wear clothes at that time, because only the adults had cloth. When I was ten years old they tore me off a piece of cloth but I didn't wrap my cloth around my waist; I usually hung it round my neck while I played. Sometimes I'd leave that cloth somewhere and my brother would go and look for it. At that time cloth was hard to come by, although it only cost two shillings a piece. You could never pay that nowadays, and it costs me twenty dollars when I buy a cloth for my wife.[3]

When we moved to Gwa'irufa it wasn't long before father left us and went to work on the plantations on Guadalcanal.

2 The taro stems, a light burden for a child, are re-planted for a future crop.

3 Solomon Islands currency changed from pounds, shillings and pence to dollars and cents in the late 1970s.

The place was called Lafuro, near Lambi Bay on West Guadalcanal, forty kilometres from Honiara. So then I was left with my two sisters and my brother Maniramo. My brother John Maesatana had gone away while I was still small to work on the plantations for Levers,[4] and he'd forgotten us. He didn't send us any money either. Before much longer my sister Filistus Sango'iburi married Alasa'a, the son of Ramo'itolo; her first marriage. She ran away with him and left us behind. Only my brother Maniramo and my small sister Ivery Arana were left, and we were all helpless.

When I was small I used to stay with Ramo'itolo, among the pagans, when my father was away. My sisters stayed at home and I went there by myself, because Alasa'a was fond of me; he was my cousin. I'd go and live with him for weeks at a time, in paganism. This was after my mother died, while we were living with Manilofia at Fa'ibeabea, along by the stream in Latea, the Ba'ufa stream with the big *rufa* trees. The Ba'ufa was their stream and in the past it was very tabu for women to go there because the men would bathe in it.[5] What I remember about Ramo'itolo when I stayed with him, was that their village had just three houses. There was the men's house, then Ramo'itolo's house higher up behind the men's house, then the women's house where the food was made, the dwelling house.

Ramo'itolo was one man who was very tabu. I remember when some Christian boys came up one evening and one of them called Siofa'a saw him holding a parcel of ginger to mix

---

4 The transnational company Levers was then the largest company running coconut plantations in Solomon Islands, using mainly Malaitan labour.

5 Under the traditional religion, the support and protection of the ghosts depended upon men avoiding defilement by women, which could have occurred if the women bathed upstream from them.

with his betelnut paste to make it taste hot.⁶ They came along
thinking these people were like the Christians, undisciplined,
because they were just undisciplined boys themselves. They
were making fun of him; 'Eh grandad, what's that you're
holding? A parcel of shit?' That's how he talked, crazy.
When he said that, Alasa'a heard and jumped at him; 'You
give me a ten-string shell money! Why are you swearing at my
father? You're saying bad things to my father, and he's a
priest for the ghosts!' Ramo'itolo demanded the shell money
and they gave it to him because he'd sworn at him.⁷

Once a child of Ramo'itolo's son So'ai was near death, at
dusk, and they took him to the mission hospital at Nāfinua.
Sango'iburi and everyone went, but I thought I'd stay with
Alasa'a and Takangwane, his brother, and Ramo'itolo. What
a surprise! After we were there a while Ramo'itolo prayed to
the ghosts and the ghost said 'Get a pig and offer it to me and
the child will get well'. He went into his house and he must
have had a vision; he said the ghost had told him that if we
did that the child would get well. He spoke from over there
and Alasa'a told me. What he said was 'We're all going to
leave you. You just stay inside the house and we'll go and
offer this sacrifice to the ghost.' They'd told all the children
to go away; 'You'll have to stay here by yourself'. Well, that
really made me tremble; 'They're all leaving me; what's going
to happen?' So I stayed all by myself in the house and when
they'd all gone I realised how hard the ghosts could be.

6 'Betelnut', the fruit of the areca palm, is a mild narcotic usually chewed
with leaves of the betel pepper vine and lime from burnt coral.

7 The 'ten-string' (*tafuli'ae*), a large-denomination 'red money', was required
as restitution (*fa'aābu'a*) for an insult which was offensive not only to
Ramo'itolo but also to his ancestral ghosts, who might have caused sickness
or death to the priest or his family if not appeased in this way. The
Christian boys appear 'undisciplined' (*dalafa*) in contrast to the strict rules
of tabu on such things observed by followers of the traditional religion.

They lived there while we grew up, but when we moved away we used to come back to shell nuts, where the nut trees grew, and we stayed in Latea.[8] This man Alasa'a was always climbing the nut trees for us, and my sister Sango'iburi always came to pick up the nuts to shell them, until the two of them made friends. Then he took her from us and ran off with her. So my father took some shell money from him; ten red shell moneys, from Alasa'a junior. He was my father's namesake and my father had named him.[9]

Well, to us the marriage between these two was wrong, according to tradition. Alasa'a junior was the son of my father's sister Siumalefo, so Sango'iburi had run away with my father's nephew. Siumalefo and my father were born of the same father and mother. Ramo'itolo married her and begot Alasa'a junior, and my father begot Sango'iburi. These two broke tradition when they took each other and that may be why it wasn't long before Alasa'a died. He died of cancer or TB, because he smoked a lot. When he took her they went to live in Latea and after a while he died leaving three children, all girls. So we took his widow back, because there was no-one to look after her, in 1966. Alasa'a's father Ramo'itolo was the last priest of Latea, and when he died everyone else joined the church.

When Sango'iburi married there was just me and my little sister Arana and Maniramo left there. That brother of mine Maniramo broke our traditional rules because he just used to go back to Anomalao and stay with relatives there and not think about us. My sister was only a little girl. We all lived in

8 People sometimes camp near their trees during the nut season. Latea is the clan-land of Ramo'itolo's family.

9 People are often named after older relatives and referred to as 'small'. 'Alasa'a junior' translates *Alasa'ate'e*; 'small Alasa'a', as distinct from *Alasa'adoe*, 'big Alasa'a', Kwa'ioloa's father.

our own house, built by Maniramo, but he was someone who didn't know how to build houses and had no idea about making anything. He built a small house which would make a lot of kitchens look good. If I'd been grown up I would never have lived in a house like that, with walls of bamboo which were all crooked and sago-leaf thatch which you could almost see the sky through. But what could we do?

I remember when Maniramo went off and left me and Arana behind, we often went hungry. We were helpless. When he went to stay in other villages he didn't think how we'd feel in the evenings. I wished my father would come back, thinking how hard things were, with no food in the house, no firewood, and the two of us unable to do anything. Sometimes in the evenings we'd go to our garden and get the sweet potatoes which grew where they'd already pulled up the potato vines. We'd dig up those potatoes and bring them home to cook, but they weren't any good. Those were hard times. We'd bring back bunches of greens and cook them in a pot, and the pot wasn't much good either. We were helpless. Even when we saw nice food in other houses we couldn't eat it. Often they wouldn't share their food with us. We'd see good things like rice and meat and fish from the market, but we couldn't eat anything like that. Sometimes Arana would ask me for something nice to eat but I couldn't do anything because I was just a child. We had a very hard time.

I remember one day, on the Easter holiday, everyone in the village went to look for fish in the A'arai river, and we really wanted some fish but what could we do? There was no-one to catch fish for us. We just took a small rusty cooking-pot and went down to the river, following them and turning over the stones one after another, looking for the small shellfish called *mengo*. But we couldn't go where the water was flowing because the current was too strong. We were really hungry that day and we found a fish, and I know it was because God in Heaven took pity on us. We saw a man kill a big fish, which seems to have escaped before it died. We saw it as we passed by and although I wasn't very big or strong I threw a big knife at it, but it was already dead. So I jumped into the water and it almost swept me away, but that little sister of mine Arana was so happy. We carried the fish back to the village, cooked it and ate it. But when we got back to our house that evening, being children, we couldn't do things properly and we had no sweet potatoes. I remember thinking 'We should eat this fish with potatoes', and then I forced my sister Arana, who was very little, to take a small bag, and I took a knife, and we went to the garden. But when we reached our garden it was all overgrown and there was no food there. We went and found the old gardens which had been cleared long before, where some potatoes had just come up later, useless ones. So we pulled up some potatoes to eat but when we got back to the house and cooked them they were no good. It's sad, but that period of my life was really hard.

Sometimes Maniramo would call in to see us, but he'd sleep for one night and then go back and stay with the other boys of his age who he played around with at Anomalao. But I remember my aunt Hilda 'Uirala, who died a long time ago now, often helped us with food. When we went to our garden she'd dig up food for us and feed us, cooking taro and sweet potatoes for us during the day. In the evening when we came home with some potatoes we were both so happy. I believe God was working miracles because he knew that one day I would work for him.

While we lived like this, the two of us would sleep at night under one blanket and we were really frightened, afraid of the dark and frightened of ghosts. There was one old man who often played jokes on us at night, pretending to be a ghost. He'd come and scratch at the walls of our house and then he'd make a strange sound like a moan. When he did that we really were frightened. The two of us would huddle together under the blanket, me and my sister, wanting to cry. Sometimes I just couldn't sleep all night. The little one would sleep but I'd just sit there, sometimes blowing on the fire, and feeling frightened. Life really was very bad at that time.

But one lonely evening the two of us lay down and night fell and towards the middle of the night a man called my name from the door. I said 'Oh, I think someone's come to kill us'. So I just went and looked through a small hole between the bamboos and saw a man carrying a heavy load on his back. Then as I looked and listened, it was my father's voice. With that I opened the door and my father brought in his bundle, wrapped in a leaf mat the way women carry things, with a bag of rice. When he unwrapped it I saw tinned meat, sugar, biscuits and all kinds of good things which my father had brought. There was a new pot and all sorts of things. Then we were happy again, and father cried with both of us. Well, he'd brought some rice and plates and things and we began to live again after that. Once father had come everyone began to be kind to us again. After that we just lived happily with my father, having a good life and enjoying ourselves, because my father had come home.

Then after father had come back he sent me to school, to get an education. By then I was about twelve years old and quite big. I went to school at Gwaunamanu for Standard One and Standard Two, and they gave me a pass. That was for two years, and then they sent me to another school at Gwa'igeo in West Kwara'ae. I was happy and said 'Oh, now I'm educated!'. I compared myself with the other children whose fathers were wealthy but who were lazy at school, so when I came home in the holidays they were far behind. That really improved my life, because I was going on to Standard Three even though they'd all failed. That made me even more pleased.

Everyone praised me and I continued with my schooling, but while I was still a small boy in my first year of Standard Three at Gwa'igeo school my father came to visit me, and when he went home I ran away after him. I couldn't stay there by myself. So I ran to a place not far away and came along behind him, and if I thought he was going to look back I hid. After we'd gone many miles I showed myself to my father, in the central bush[10] near Osifera's village at a place called Fauso'obobo, midway between East and West. By then it was hard for father to take me back so he took me with him, but he beat me. He said, 'Do you want to be like me, not knowing anything?', but I said 'We live on food, father. We don't live on education.' Although I was only small, what I said to my father made him sorry for me and he took me back to live at home. I stayed there several years, until they sent me back to school at Gwaunafau, at Standard Three again.[11]

When we went to school we studied, but you know what it was like at school in those days, leaving your mother and father. My body was in class, but my mind was with my father. So I didn't get a good education then because in my heart I didn't have the things I wanted. When I tried it that time I more or less gave up and stayed home until I grew up.

10 'Bush' (Pijin *bus*) is the common expression for 'inland' (Kwara'ae *tolo*), 'central bush' being the mountainous interior of the island.

11 Gwaunafau is in East Kwara'ae, close enough to Kwa'ioloa's home for him to attend as a day-pupil.

Guadalcanal and Honiara, showing roads and some of the places mentioned in this book.

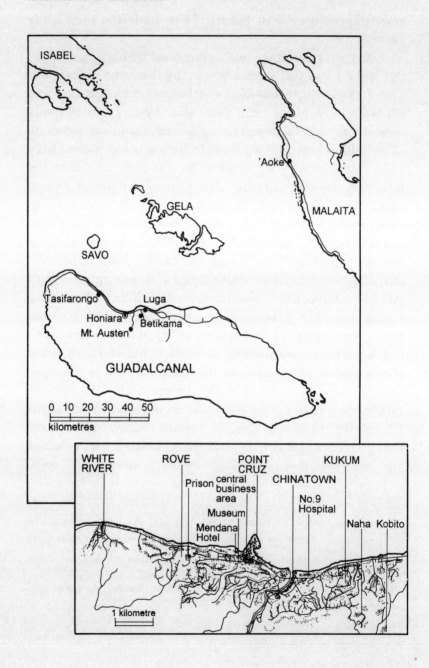

3 Going to Town

I've already told how my brother John Maesatana left us, before I can remember, to go to the plantations. They used to go to Gizo to places like Tetebari, belonging to Levers, to try and get some money. It wasn't easy to get money at home because our elders wouldn't allow any companies to start work there. They stopped them, they said, because of tradition. When they used to go to the plantations they thought the work was all right, but the men who ran the plantations in those days, they used to say how violent they were. If they saw the workers slacking a bit, there'd be a boot in the backside. That's the kind they were; some of them would beat the men up, those European bosses on the plantations.

For this reason, when Honiara began to grow people came to work clearing the brush.[1] But in the past Honiara was a difficult place for Malaitans to get to, so only very few people came. When they came to clear the brush some helped with other work until eventually the town began to develop and things got better. Some went into the stores, some began to join building firms, and more and more companies came to Honiara to build up the town. Then they began to take on labourers to dig foundations, to work on trucks shovelling sand and gravel for building. They needed more and more labour and as a result, if someone came back at Christmas, everyone at home would say 'Eh, he's a Honiara man, that's what he is!' They'd see all the good things he had; maybe he'd bring tins of meat, maybe some rice, and they'd say 'All right, when you go back we'll both go together.' Everyone was like that with their relatives, and when they arrived they all set to work. They knew the work was easy, and those who continued going

1 The capital of Solomon Islands had been moved to Honiara after the Second World War, established on the site of an American wartime base.

to the plantations to cut copra were mainly the Kwaio, and some Kwara'ae. That's because life was hard working for Levers, and the money wasn't very good either.[2]

Then in 1965 my brother John Maesatana married a girl in Honiara, so my father Samuel Alasa'a took five ten-string shell moneys, and I cried as he left, so my father took me to Honiara. John Maesatana had written a letter saying 'I'm marrying a girl. Bring some shell money, because they're waiting for it.' Our tradition is that a girl must be paid for with red shell money. The father was a good man, so he only demanded five ten-string moneys.[3] So, my father took five ten-strings and the two of us travelled inland and down to 'Aoke. That was the first time I'd seen 'Aoke.[4] When I got there it was quite a surprise; 'Eh, look at all those big stores!' My father went to buy a small tin of fish from a store belonging to a Chinese called Siulae and it cost one shilling and sixpence. I thought that was a lot of money. The passage on the ship to Honiara cost thirteen shillings, but I went free because I was just a child. But those ships were the kind where you held a tiller to steer by. The ship took something like eight hours to reach Honiara, or even ten. It was called the *Waikiki* and it was a cutter belonging to a Kwara'ae man called Cornelius Kono. When we set out for Honiara I

2   Kwaio, immediately to the south of Kwara'ae, includes some of the most isolated and culturally conservative communities in Solomon Islands, whose men usually lack the education to get anything but the least rewarding jobs in the capitalist economy.

3   Five large denomination 'red moneys' such as ten-string *tafuli'ae* is the standard bridewealth (paid by the husband's family to the wife's family) approved by most Malaitan churches. But in the past the amount was negotiable and some people still demand more.

4   'Aoke (or Auki as it is often mis-spelled) is the administrative capital of Malaita, on the west coast of Kwara'ae, the opposite side of the island to Kwa'ioloa's home.

thought it was a really distant place, because it took us all day. I watched Savo Island and it seemed to stay in the same place. I got hungry on the ship, but when I thought it was a long way it was just because the ship hardly moved. Things were difficult in those days and there weren't any good ships.

When we reached Honiara my father paid for the girl for my brother John Maesatana, and when my father went back to Malaita I didn't want to go. It was my first time in Honiara and when I came to live there I ate bread, my brother bought meat and I ate that, he bought shorts and I wore them, and I was really happy. That was the first time I'd ever had those things. So I said 'Father, maybe you should go and I'll stay with my brother for a bit.' I was sleeping on a mat too! All this was so different from the way I'd lived on Malaita. While I was living with my brother one strange thing I did was to hold money in my own hands for the first time. When my sister-in-law went to do the washing for my brother, while he was at work, I went with her to carry the plates. I saw some coins she'd taken from my brother's pocket and I took them thinking they'd float. So I put them in the stream to float them, but they just sank! I tried it again and again until my sister-in-law Betelin Gwalata said 'Michael, whatever are you doing?' I said 'Well, I thought money would float.' She could see I was someone who knew nothing about money. That was the first time I ever held money.

Back in 1965 when my father and me came to Honiara, there was no Kobito village there.[5] No, the place where Kobito is, where all those houses are, was a thick jungle, a home for wild pigs. And the stream at Kobito which they now throw rubbish in and which sometimes dries up in hot

5 Kobito is one of many 'urban villages', originally squatter settlements on the outskirts of town, where most of the Malaitan residents of Honiara now live in largely self-governing communities.

weather, I wasn't big enough to bathe in it because the pools were so deep, with eels in them, like the big stream at home at A'arai. My brother's house was the only one there and when all us Malaitans came to work there were all my big brothers in the house of my brother John Maesatana above the path. At that time the land wasn't bought or rented and the government hadn't yet made us pay for the land. A brother of mine, Kaobata, had been living there at his garden and when he went to work for Mr Secombe, a Jehovah's Witness, at Coral Industries, he went down to live in the town and gave the house to my brother.

So when my fathers and brothers came from Malaita they all lived in the one house. While I was there I remember us having twenty-five plates at a meal. They put the greens in one big pot and it was like having a party at the house, there were so many of us. But there was no shortage of food because with that land you just had to plant sweet potatoes and there was the food. Just imagine twenty-five people or more working in a garden on a weekend. Where the hills are now just covered with grass, it was probably us who ruined them. They cut down the thick jungle and planted sweet potatoes, tapioca, greens and things like beans and tomatoes; my word, we were rich in food. On a Saturday if they all went there they'd bring back ten or fifteen sacks, each man carrying a sack, and we were really rich in food. Sometimes my brother would dig food to sell to Number Nine hospital[6] or to pig farms, so we got money from it too.

That's how I remember it before there was a village there. It started to grow when the people staying in my brother's house began to say 'Oh, maybe I'll build a house here so I can bring my wife over.' So one after another they began to build their own houses and bring their wives and as they worked and

6 Number Nine is Honiara's hospital, named after a wartime installation.

others went to live with them my brother's house emptied out. As they spread out into separate houses it made more people come; 'Oh, I'll go to stay with my brother in Honiara.' They'd come, stay a while, work for two or three months, and build a house too. Eventually there was a town at Kobito, and now there are almost seventy houses in Kobito One and Two. They've left Malaita and come to Honiara for money to support their families, because there's increasing development, there are schools, children need clothes and there are school fees to pay. And then there were some who wanted to run hawker-stores to sell a few tins of meat at home, so they came too.[7] Buying axes and kitchen utensils such as saucepans and knives; all this made people come.

When I went there my life was changed. Yes, I thought back to when I lived at home and when I compared it I didn't want to go home. I wanted to go on living in town. Because in Honiara I really enjoyed walking along the nice streets and going into the big stores which I'd never seen before. That was with my brother; I couldn't go by myself because I didn't know how to cross the road and things like that. My brother went around showing me everything and all the things I saw in the stores looked very strange. At that time it was six boxes of matches for one shilling. That was very good, but now it's thirty cents a box. It was three shillings for one big tin of 777 fish; now it's seven dollars, one shilling for a stick of tobacco; now it's almost two dollars. In those days money was limited but it was worth more.[8] Another thing I saw at that time were the trucks, and I went in a truck too, because my brother was working for a company and I always went in the truck with

7 Village stores, not actually hawkers but named after the government 'hawker licence' required for small-scale retailing in the rural areas.

8 One Solomon Islands dollar is equivalent to ten shillings in the old currency. Solomon Islands suffers continual and increasing inflation.

him. I was so happy. I saw it all there, all the men in nice clothes working in the offices; it was all new to me.

Before that, when I thought about the town I used to say 'What's town?' It was hard for me to understand what town was, because it was a European word. But when I got there I said 'Oh, town's a big village, but a very nice looking village.' So then I understood about town. I didn't know about town because on Malaita our houses were built on the ground, without floors in the past, just enclosed with bamboos, and we just used tree bark for doors and tree bark to lie down on beside the fire. I didn't see anyone who had nice things either. If a man with a wristwatch came to Malaita everyone came to look at it. They were hard to come by, and everything else was difficult too. But when I reached Honiara I saw life had changed and I didn't want Malaita any more. So I stayed there, went to school there, rode a bicycle, and really enjoyed myself.

In 1966 my brother sent me to the Seventh Day Adventist school at Burns Creek, near Luga bridge. He took me there and they tested me; 'Well, how much does this boy know?' My brother said 'I don't know, because he's been educated all over the place.' So they tested my knowledge and I had to go in at Standard Four. When they put me at Standard Four in the SDA school I really thought I was somebody! My brother bought me a uniform, for the first time in my life, and bought me a towel and all sorts of good things.

While I was at that school I had a hard time getting there. I had to go by foot all the way from Kobito to Burns Creek and back again, because it was a day school. So when I found it difficult my brother said 'Oh, you'll have to learn how to ride a bicycle.' So I tried hard learning how to ride, until I damaged my brother Fa'abasua's bicycle by riding it over the open ground. It was his way of getting to work too, and I damaged it quite badly. But when I really knew how to ride a bicycle my brother bought a *New London* bicycle for me. It was my first time to own a bicycle and I think I was the first one in the neighbourhood to have one. I was just a child of about fourteen, and my brother Maesatana bought the bicycle for thirteen pounds. It was second hand from a dental mechanic, my uncle Kwasi, Daurara's son. I still remember how I couldn't sleep at night, it was so exciting to be able to ride the bicycle the next day. I'd touch the bicycle a few times during the night and say 'Morning come quickly, so I can use my bicycle!' I'd lie down for a bit and then touch the bicycle again.

But I didn't yet understand how to ride a bicycle around town, because my home was situated on the edge of town. Every day I had to travel east but the town was to the west and it was crowded with trucks and lots of bicycles and people walking around. Some of them drove carelessly, so my brother said 'Don't go there.' My brother paid for the registration of the bicycle with the Town Council. It cost five shillings and they stamped a metal strap and put it on the bicycle, under the saddle. I was surprised we had to pay five shillings registration for a bicycle, but that was the law of the Town Council; nowadays you don't have to do it. And when I rode the bicycle everyone was surprised too; 'Eh, you're a lucky man having a bicycle.' My life had really improved by then and when I compared it with the past, when my mother died and I was looked after by other people, my eyes filled with tears.

So I went on with school and passed Standard Five, and they sent me on to Betikama Adventist High School. While I was there for Standard Six it was my first time to be taught by a European. At Standard Four and Standard Five I was only taught by the one person, but at Standard Six everyone taught me. Each European had to take the class for certain periods, for the subject he taught. So I learnt from each person and saw each one's face and heard his voice. That really helped me to learn English and learn how to write, because among all those teachers were some who were very good. When they were explaining something in detail they used to call me Mr Question in the class. I was always asking questions, because I was comparing things with my previous life when everything was hard, and as I grew older I just had to ask questions. All this questioning made me good in class and I was confident too, so they told me to be the class prefect. When the teachers went out it was me who sat up there and watched over the others, and when I looked at myself I said 'Oh, now I am doing well!' That motivated me even more, and when I got to Standard Seven the headmaster or Principal came to teach us. He was Mr Ward, a man from Australia. I was lucky because during the year I was in Standard Seven this Mr Ward took me for six months, and when it was time for him to go back to Australia another European came, Mr Smith from New Zealand. That means I was taught by two different men, and I got even more experience from that.

So I was doing well in my education, but some business over a girl put an end to it. They sacked me. This girl business was during the holidays, out of school, and you know what it's like when you're young. I had a girlfriend, out of school, and someone outside reported me to the school. Someone phoned and told them and then they tried to find out whether I was guilty or not, and I tried to make out I wasn't guilty. But actually I'd done it. At the faculty meeting they asked me 'Well, did you do such and such, while you were on holiday?' I didn't try to deny it or anything, but I said 'Eh, this is a thing which should be outside of the school. If it was in the school, okay.' But there you are; they didn't agree with me because that was the constitution or policy of the school. If anyone messed around out of school or came to school and didn't follow the school rules, he was out. So I tried the religious line, as a person from the SSEC who'd come under the SDA. 'Well, am I not one of your sheep, coming as one lost? If you'll forgive me I'll go ahead and do my best to stay at school until the end, because my brother has paid a lot for the fees.' But they just refused, and I know it was from prejudice. Because there was another boy from Western Solomons in the same trouble as me, but he belonged to the SDA and they allowed him to stay while they sacked me. I hadn't joined the SDA because I didn't believe in it and because religious and spiritual matters didn't interest me. So I finished school with the sack.

Back in those days, in 1971, Standard Seven leavers held big jobs in government, and I had enough education to get a job. When I left school the first place I went to look for work was the Youth Club, and they made me a barman. While I was in the bar my salary (in dollars by that time) was eighteen dollars a month, which was a lot. I worked well and everything was cheap so that was all right, but then two of my brothers who were members of the club came along. They always used credit, running up an account till the end of the week, and if they didn't pay it off I was the one who had to pay it back, and they'd cut my wages. I didn't like that, so I got out.

Because in our way of life giving support to relatives is very important. For me, if I want to support one of my brothers it's very simple, not a difficult thing to do. I'll just get some money and give it to him. With us, a man who needs a pig can just come and ask. He'll say 'Just help me out with a pig.' I saw my fathers do it. Then when I've helped him and he's used the pig for someone's wedding, he'll give back another pig. Even if he doesn't come to ask me, if I hear that my brother's son is marrying a girl and going to pay for her, I have to take a ten-string shell money and pay for her. And when I've paid for the girl I won't ask my brother to help me with my ordinary needs but only for wedding expenses. He has to wait till one of my children gets married before he stands by me as I did for him and his son. Then he'll bring another ten-string shell money and give it to help me. But we don't keep an account of it; we're just supporting each other. That's what was going on in the minds of my two brothers, Maelasi and Sisi. They'd always come to drink until it came to the end of the month, and then; nothing. Then, even though my wages were cut, when I asked them they'd say, 'Oh, you understand.' And because of our old way of helping our brothers I wasn't angry. I said 'Oh, this is getting difficult, I'll just stop.' So I lost a good job at the Youth Club.

It wasn't that those two intended to spoil things for me. After our fashion, they thought they'd help me out another time, when we were drinking. Because at that time I used to drink beer too. Drinking beer was my main interest. They thought 'If you help us now when we're short of money, next time, at the end of the month or whenever, we'll all come along and drink and we two will pay for the beer.' I agreed to that because our way was, when we got together at a hotel, if we were brothers one would pay for the beer and we'd sit down together and drink. But the problem was that while we were enjoying a drink in the public bar, if a man didn't keep control of himself and lost his senses he'd empty his pockets. He'd take out all the money he had and ask the barman to send over a full crate. Then as we drank some of us were in luck and kept our money. Sometimes we'd try to stop him too; 'Eh, just spend a bit, or when our turn comes we won't get the chance!' And then he'd show off and empty his pockets. Sometimes he'd give us all the money left over too. He'd hold out his hand; 'Eh, take the money! Take it for yourself!' Because he couldn't control himself. When that happened we'd just take him out, get a taxi and go and leave him at his house.

I only got into all this drinking while I was working in the club. Otherwise it would have been very difficult for me, because I didn't even know what drinking beer was. I didn't know about town ways. It was from working in the commercial centre of Honiara that I learnt about that, and it was only when I started working that I learnt how to smoke. When I first started smoking it was unpleasant, but I did it again and again until I knew how to do it. Because I had lots of friends who smoked and they made me smoke too, and drink beer. I went around with the young boys in town, and they also took me to the cinema to watch movies; moving pictures. In the first movie I ever watched I saw Elvis Presley. It awed me too, to see such a good-looking boy playing the guitar, with all the girls gathering around him. When I saw that I really was in awe! Even the Queen's daughter cried for that man Elvis Presley. He was a popular singer all round the world, the king of pop music.

While my brothers were leading me into these things and I was getting interested, they also took me to clubs to dance. I'll just explain about the girls who came out to dance with us. They were girls with clerical jobs in the town who lived in hostels. They paid them to come to the dance and whether they were girls or married women and even if you were a young boy, you'd dance with them. Because they'd been paid to come they were willing to dance with anyone. So the first night I went to a dance, I just sat down while the music was playing and a girl came over. All the girls came and took the boys by the hand, and a Fijian woman took my hand, so I decided to dance with her. I didn't know any of the women, but she was a young woman so I said 'Oh, it's only a dance.' According to tradition it's tabu, but I wanted to do it anyway, so I went ahead. I was holding a cigarette which was still alight, and we had our arms round one another in a slow-motion dance. We took one step, then another, to the slow-motion music. Then as I pressed up against her my cigarette burnt her on the breast and she got angry with me; 'Eh, if you weren't so interested in that cigarette you'd have more luck with me!' That made me feel bad, and I said 'I'm thinking too much about smoking.'

That was my first time to see all that, and to hold a girl, because my father had told me that girls were tabu.[9] You mustn't hold a girl belonging to a man. But after my first lapse, when I was at school and I lost my education, I got angry with myself and I said 'If I'm going to go wrong, I might as well go wrong.' So when I got into all this, I saw those girls and I had to dance with them. I'd even spoilt my education; that's why I was willing to hold that woman. I hadn't expected to dance with her either, because when we gathered there all us men were sitting down on one side and all the women were on the other side. With us, things to do with girls are very difficult, such as holding another woman. But when I joined the others and held different women it led me into another way of life. We call it being undisciplined.[10] I knew I was wrong because my culture forbids it, but I'd followed the fashion and become the kind of person with a town lifestyle. So I went dancing time after time and I used to watch along the street for any posters they put up saying 'Big Midnight Dance at such and such a hotel'. It cost me five shillings for a ticket to go in at that time, and then when I

9 Tabu (Kwara'ae *ābu*) in this sense means that girls and women must be protected from sexual advances, which would spoil their reputations and offend their menfolk.

10 Kwa'ioloa uses the Pijin word *enihao* to translate Kwara'ae *maladalafa*, which means ignoring or disrespecting the proper rules of social behaviour and tabu, and hence being unworthy of respect yourself.

danced with a woman I'd have to buy us both drinks, which was worse, and by the end I'd have run out of money.

While this was going on, my brother got me interested in music, and I started to play the guitar. There was a group called The Echoes, with David Totori as the singer and Hudson Fa'arodo as the lead guitar. That was the first time I saw entertainers, and they used electric guitars; Solomon Islanders. They were my brothers too, and David Totori was a boy from 'Are'are in South Malaita; he sang like Elvis Presley. One place I went to, at the weekend at the end of every month, was the Gilbertese Club at White River.[11] I was a member there, and that's where I joined up with the others to play music. Then Rocky Hardy Tisa started to compose music and I helped him as a back-up singer, for worldly songs. He didn't sing in church; he just sang about girls, about nature, about the rivers, about the town, about drinking. Those were things I understood too.

Rocky Hardy Tisa is my nephew, son of my sister Alari'i.[12] (Alari'i was born of Sareto'ona and I was born of Alasa'a, two clan brothers). When he asked me to be his back-up singer we were playing local style, and it was the first time I'd used an amplifier. John Maetia, who became a government Minister, gave us the amplifier. When we started playing to entertain for parties back at home it was the first time the local people had seen guitars. That was later, when I went back home to try and change my life, but before that we began by practising with our brothers in Honiara. We played in the studio of

11 Belonging to Gilbert Islands immigrants, many of whom live in the White River suburb to the west of Honiara.

12 Nephew and uncle both translate *ngwai*, which means both mother's brother and sister's son.

SIBC[13] too, at that time. Although I was interested in music it was only local style and I didn't really know how to handle a guitar, and nor did Rocky. But eventually Rocky Hardy Tisa became well-known from singing the songs he composed, *Faumamanu Market*, which the two of us used to sing, and then *Hibiscus Garu* and *Blue Bungana*, which are still popular now. He earned some money from it by making a contract with SIBC. But not me; I'm just telling how I joined up with him.

When I left the Youth Club bar I went to look for work and got a job at Tasifarongo, a plantation in west Guadalcanal. I was a stockman, and it was the first time I rode a horse. When I was learning to ride I was always falling off and the horse would almost step on me, but I tried again and again. And when I saddled the horse by myself I wouldn't fasten the buckles well and sometimes when I'd been riding for a while the buckles would come undone and me and the saddle would both fall off. But I tried again and again and learnt how to ride a horse and became good at it.

When I was little I didn't know what fighting was either, or quarrelling and things like that. When I was in Malaita all I saw was the older men quarrelling about something, then settling it. While I was living at Anomalao I remember how a cousin of mine, Leka'i, once made a girl pregnant, a pagan girl called Maeta. So they came to ask for shell money and Leka'i refused it and, being wild people, they fought, but they didn't use weapons. They just hit each other with their fists and the people in the village got hold of them, some holding one side, some the other, and they took them away and talked. They paid for the girl seven days later, shook hands

13 The Solomon Islands Broadcasting Corporation, which operates the national radio station and publishes local music from its recording studios.

and that was the end of it; there was peace.[14] That was the
first time I saw fighting, among my fathers, but it wasn't
serious fighting and they weren't enemies. It was just a row,
and they held each other back.

When I went to town I didn't do things like that, because
I was afraid. But I remember one Friday while I was working
at Tasifarongo, my brothers Sisi and Maelasi took me back to
town to drink. We drank until late in the night and a group
from another district of Malaita came and challenged us in the
hotel, so there was a fight. We were in the public bar of the
Mendana Hotel[15] and six young boys like ourselves came
looking for a fight. That was my first time; 'Eh, I'm in a fight!
What am I going to do?' It was the first time in my life I'd
ever got into fighting, and I realised I was in town and I was a
hooligan. I was in a corner of the bar and while I was sitting
there they came and tried to make a challenge. They were
asking if anyone wanted a fight. It was just drunkenness; you
know these hooligans. They just came and said 'Who cares
about you lot?' Then one man took a punch at my brother
Sisi's beer and at the same time I saw the other one, Maelasi,
who was sitting next to him, take a full unopened bottle of
beer and bash it against the side of the man's head. So the
man fell down and when they saw that they got scared and
gave up looking for a fight and walked out. They asked for
their man and went, but he was wounded on the side of the
head. It was the first time I'd seen a fight.

The next night, on Saturday, I went to drink by myself in
the Mendana Hotel. I drank until I lost my senses, and the
public bar closed at ten o'clock. When it was nearly ten

14 That is, bridewealth was given and the couple were married.

15 The Mendana is the smartest hotel in Honiara where, as in other hotels,
ordinary islanders were normally allowed to drink only in the public bar,
partly for reasons obvious from this incident.

o'clock they said 'Okay, buy your last beers', so that night, before the bar closed, I bought a pack of six beers, opened them all and took them and went out. I thought I was going up to Kukum, to the east, but I went west, because I'd lost my senses. I was staying at Kukum at the Labour-lines with my brother, for the weekend.[16] It was the Labour-line of the Express Building Company, a company from Australia. So instead of walking east I went back west to Rove. I thought I was safely home but as I went on I felt ill and I didn't know what I was doing. I lost my senses, so I sat down at the bottom of a Christmas tree[17] and lay down and went to sleep. I said 'I'm home' but I didn't know what I was doing; it was the first time I'd been in that disgraceful state. As I slept all the beer poured out into my jacket and made me all wet. Eventually, towards dawn, I felt cold and shook, 'Eh!', and I saw the street light. I said 'Eh' and looked around me; 'My word, I'm dead! Someone must have cut me up with a knife.' So I started back to Kukum, and my watch said four o'clock. I went up Hibiscus Avenue and round the Police Station, in case they caught me, and I ran back to Kukum. By the time I reached Kukum it was five o'clock in the morning.

That was the first time I'd got into that kind of life, and when I came back to the house and sat down I felt guilty about it. I remembered my father and thought about it hard and I said 'I'll have to get out of that job at Tasifarongo, with the cattle. I ought to come and work here, with my brother in the Express Company.' The job at Tasifarongo was good, but it was because I didn't want to be with my two brothers. I was still of good character and I had to escape from them so I wouldn't be led astray. When I first got to Tasifarongo I

16 'Labour-lines' are the standardised housing built for migrant workers.

17 'Christmas tree' is a local name for the introduced Flame of the Forest tree, which bears its bright red flowers around that time of the year.

didn't know what stealing was either, but those two brothers got us to steal a pig belonging to a Guadalcanal man. We went by night to take the man's pig, just took it and ate it. These things were making me feel guilty and when I thought about it I remembered my father, because he was a chief who'd told me what to do. When I thought about him I was really sorry, so I tried to be good again. I said 'I'll have to leave those two.'

These things had taken my life far from the old ways I'd followed at home. I'd heard what my father said and I hadn't done it, but when I went off like that I knew what I was doing was wrong. My father told me when I was little that those things I was doing were bad. I should have lived a traditional way of life, but while I was living in town I forgot my traditional ways. As far as fighting was concerned, my father told me I mustn't fight. If I fight, according to tradition, I won't live long because enemies will cut my life short. I won't have good friends to help when something happens to me, and when I'm paying for a girl or making a feast some of my relatives might not want to help me. That's why my father said 'You must live a peaceful life, to please everyone in the neighbourhood and at the same time make people respect you.' If I fought they wouldn't respect me, and besides it was important because I was the son of a chief; if I got involved in the kind of thing I'd been doing it would bring down his good name; 'What kind of chief's son does things like that?' All this made me think about changing my way of life.

4　The Power of Ghosts and God

When I got the urge to join in these kinds of things, it didn't come out of nowhere. Because while I was working at Tasifarongo, and I'd left my brother's family to live by myself, one night I dreamed of my dead mother Arana. She came and spoke to me; 'Be careful my son, if you don't look to me they'll kill you.' When I woke up I thought it was real, but it was just a dream. But the next night a strange thing happened; she came and explained everything to me. 'Well, my son, from now on you'll be with me. But don't go under floors where women are above, don't go under lines where they've hung up women's clothes, and don't eat with women who are having their monthly periods, or go near childbirth.'[1] She told me all this.

This is something in my blood. In traditional times the same thing happened to the ancestors, especially when you left Malaita and went to live on another island. For example, when you got lost at sea you'd think of your ghosts. You'd tremble and a shark would come and lift you out of the water onto its back and swim with you and leave you on the shore, even if you were somewhere you couldn't see an island.[2] So that's what happened when I was losing direction in life and my mother appeared to me. It's traditional, and in our tradition if a man needs a ghost he has to concentrate his thoughts on it and make a claim. As he makes this claim he has to think about the shrines where they offer sacrifices and he has to concentrate hard in his mind and say to himself

1　These instructions to avoid defilement by women are standard rules of the traditional religion, essential for keeping men, and the ghosts who would protect them, tabu and hence spiritually strong.

2　Certain ghosts, the ancestors of coastal people in particular, were incarnated in sharks and would protect their descendants in ways like this.

Kwara'ae traditional costume, like that of the ghost encountered by
Kwa'ioloa on his night-time journey across Malaita. Aisah Osifera, the father
of Kwa'ioloa who prevented the road from going through the central bush
(see page 137), wears his pearlshell pendant, nosepin and cane belt, and
carries a *subi* club. (1984)

A church wedding, like that held for Kwa'ioloa and Fanenalua, with suit, bridal dress and bridesmaids. (from a Kwara'ae wedding photo, 1990)

Preparing a feast. The pigs have had their bristles singed on the fire and are being butchered ready for cooking in a stone oven. (1984)

Bizel Fanenalua,
Kwa'ioloa's wife,
in 1979.

Kwa'ioloa's village at Anobala in 1979, with relatives and neighbours.

Kwa'ioloa (in shirt) with his family and guests in the kitchen at Anobala in 1979. In the background is his father Alasa'a.

something like this; 'Oh, let me be with my brothers offering a sacrifice to ancestor so-and-so.' When you think like this you'll get this emotional feeling when you cry and tremble. The ancestor has come!

It's like this. When I dreamt of my mother I hadn't been thinking about this, but I had thought about her. When my brother was leading his own life mother used him and later on when he joined the church he told me the things she'd used him for, and then I thought a lot about my mother. Sometimes while I was sitting on the seashore I'd look out to sea and think about her; 'Eh, what about my mother?' I went on thinking like that until one night she appeared, because I wanted her. A thing like that should have frightened me, because she was dead, but when I saw her I wasn't afraid because she told me those interesting things. She said 'You've got me with you now, and you can depend on me for everything.' Then next morning I found five cents on my pillow and when I saw it I knew; 'Oh, it's my mother.' The five cents was the ghost, so I kept it and followed the rules she gave me.[3] I didn't go around with girls too much. I don't know why, but even though she was a woman she appeared as a ghost and that made me tabu.[4] It's traditional with us Malaitans for a man to take a ghost to give him protection when he's away at work, and it's nothing new. It's the way we are, so when my mother appeared to me and stayed with me I was very pleased.

3 In Kwara'ae the term 'ghost' (*akalo,* Pijin *defolo* or *devol*) covers not only ancestral spirits but also magical creatures, substances and objects such as the five cent coin talisman which men often receive as a symbol of a ghost's protection.

4 Kwa'ioloa is here acknowledging an apparent contradiction in the fact that women, who are defiling to ghosts and men in life, can themselves be tabu and vulnerable to feminine defilement as ghosts after death.

One strange thing she did with me was that when other people were talking about me, because I was a delinquent and they were planning to attack me, at the night while I slept she'd bring an image of them all as they sat and talked and I'd know what they were planning for me. In the dream there'd be one of you sitting in a chair here, another over there, and as you talked I'd stand there with my mother and listen. So next day when you tried to attack me, you couldn't do it. And another secret that I loved my mother for, as a ghost, was when we wanted to go and steal. When I travelled she said 'Don't hide your footprints; just walk on the ground and even if they see them it'll be all right.' I proved this when I travelled. When I went to steal or to meet a girl in some secret place, a megapode bird would call after me, a wild bird of the bush. What it did was come and scratch around so no-one could see my footprints. That was strange; when I travelled and left footprints the bird would come and do this scratching and later on if it flew in front of me it meant there were people there and it was easy for me to escape. I knew it was my mother helping me with magic again.

For instance, when we went to steal the Guadalcanal man's pig I dreamed of it at night, knowing we were going, and then I thought a bit about my mother. When we went we rode horses and we tied them up at the bottom of a big banyan tree and went in. I wasn't afraid because I knew my mother was there. I walked alone to the other side of the stream and went into the house and mother made the people sleep. They were afraid of sorcery and hadn't shut the door. When I walked inside I took some pineapples and bananas and put them in my bag, I took some money, I walked back and then we took the pig and went. I knew that even at night the megapode would cover my footprints and in the morning the man didn't know who had taken his pig.

Then there was the fighting. Once I was in the Kongsong bar, a hotel in the middle of Chinatown, when a fight broke out. A man threw a bottle at me but I saw it and jumped out of the way. As I defended myself I saw my mother standing there. The image of my mother was standing and laughing at me. Then my mother just looked and pointed at the man and I really laid into him and kicked him. And at that time everyone looked to me nothing more than a small cat. That was the power my mother was showing me. All the men were small enough for me to go and grab them by the throat and strangle them. They didn't look like men to me. My body felt powerful, light and strong, as if I was a ghost. It seemed to me as if it was mother who was striking them, and when I looked at them they were small in my eyes. So after that I knew what my brother had told me was true. That's what I did in the hotel; we beat up those men, not killing them dead but wounding them, and then we ran off. The police came but we were gone. So that also made me realise that the power of the ghost was really true for me.

I experienced the reality of my mother as a ghost if I stole from a house or wanted a girl. I wasn't really one to steal from houses, because my tradition says that a man who does that is worthless, but as for girls, I used to get them out of the house to spend time with them at night. I'm sorry to say this, but that's how I lived.[5] I'd go inside as arranged during the day and I could get through a locked door, because the power was in me. You could lock your house up but I'd come and hold the lock and blow on it. I'd think of my mother, blow 'pff' and the lock would unlock. I'd open it and go in. That was one of my mother's secrets. I've not told anyone until now,

5 Malaitans have particularly strict rules protecting the chastity of women and girls, so Kwa'ioloa's activities were quite risky, the kind of behaviour which a few generations ago could have resulted in both him and his girlfriends being killed.

but I want to put it in my story so my children can see it and compare good and bad ways of living.

This power of my mother, who Satan was using, was a really good thing. It would make some of my brothers very kind to me, and not only were they kind but they gave me good things. I know, because before I was in that situation my brothers were unkind and they weren't likely to help me with money and things. Sometimes I had friends from other islands, my own friends who bought beer for me and paid for taxis for us to go around in. There was a fast taxi which ran around Honiara which was only fifty cents for anywhere in town. So I know that the power of the ghost working through my mother was very real when I received free gifts from my friends and they bought me expensive things, and drink, and paid for me to go to movies and dances and travel around. I know it was the power of the ghost, a blessing given to me because she was my mother. That's what made everyone take an interest in me and give me things.

It was revealed in the shade[6] of my mother, but I also think there must have been another ghost acting through mother, because of what happened once when I came back from Honiara on holiday. I started from 'Aoke to travel inland into the bush, because I'd made friends with a girl at home and she'd set a time for the two of us to meet, for about ten o'clock at night. But I was busy in town because I went to visit my father at Namoraku and when I got back all the trucks which would have taken me up the 'Afi'o road had already gone. I got to 'Aoke about four o'clock, thinking about the girl, and I should have slept there but I set out on the long journey through the bush. So I bought ten boxes of

6 Kwara'ae distinguish between a person's shade (*nununa*) as an image of the person, their ghost (*akalo*) which comes into being at death, their soul or breath (*mangona*) and their spirit (*anoanona*). The exact relationship between these spiritual aspects of a person can be rather ambiguous.

matches, as there were no torches, and I took two cans of Coca-cola and some biscuits and three tins of Ma Ling luncheon meat, because I thought when I reached my friend we could have something to eat. But I was drunk too. I hailed a police truck which took me to 'Afi'o and then I set off into the bush. I'd just got into the hills when the gongs for evening service cried out, and I got worried. I went on until I reached Osifera's village at Fi'ika'o at eight o'clock, but I still didn't want to sleep there because the girl was waiting for me at ten o'clock. She'd sent a message secretly all the way to Honiara to arrange it, so it was very important. It was worrying me a lot, so I waited while Osifera gave me some taro and two or three pieces of pork and I went on. By then I was using the matches and when I felt the place I'd got to was steep or rocky I'd just strike a match, take a look, jump and go on again.

Then it happened to me. When I got to Fa'ikwa'u, a place in my own land of Siale, one of my ancestors followed me. It was a ghost, one of the old ones from long ago. He followed me and he would have killed me, because I didn't know how to speak to him. When he began to follow me I felt something was wrong. It was about half past eight so I rushed on, because it was getting near to ten o'clock, until I reached the 'Ongi pool in the central bush. After I crossed the 'Ongi I found out how strong was the power of ghosts in the Malaita bush. I came to some stone platforms made by a bush man called Maelekini as places to rest and eat, and a sound like a pig with lots of piglets came into the place, which is like a dried up stream bed. They were coming, and then the thought came to me; 'Run, run up the hill, or it'll kill you.' So I ran up the hill and that great pig came with a rushing wind and went right through the place I'd been standing, the place called Maelekini's Stone Bench. As it went past I ran up until I reached the stream called the Maeru'a. It was at Maeru'a that I had the experience, a place where long ago a warrior called

Kali used to kill people. Something enormous, maybe an eagle, came flying along the dry stream bed and I heard it making a sound like a bird's wings. So I ran up the hill again and it went downwards. I knew that ghosts were very powerful in the Malaita bush, but that was the first time I'd witnessed it.

Then I went on, with six boxes of matches finished and another four to go. Eventually I reached a place called 'Ainganga cave in the 'Ere'ere district, a kind of rock shelter. When I got there I cut four fronds from a wild betelnut palm and although my friend was waiting for me I was tired and it was ten o'clock, so I said 'Oh, forget it; I'll have to sleep here. I give up.' So I made a bit of a fire, drank a Coca-cola, lay down and slept. As I slept I dreamed that my mother had come once again. I saw her stand facing me and I saw a very old man come and stand beside her, but he wasn't looking at me, he was looking at a thicket of bamboos down the hill. He was carrying a big *subi* club on his arm and I could see he had a shell-bead armband and I could see the tip of a crescent pendant and the end of a nosepin sticking out, and he was wearing a cane belt. As my mother stood there she only came up to his buttocks, he was so tall, but he wasn't looking at me, he was looking downwards. Then my mother said 'Look at him, it's your ancestor standing here.[7] If it wasn't for mother he'd kill you. Get up and go while you're still alive.' She didn't tell me the man's name, but I was afraid of him. When I woke up I looked around and said 'I'm still frightened' but then I said 'Oh, mother's with me', so I went on. Mother had

7 Kwa'ioloa identifies this ghost with an ancestor on his father's side from Siale, who had followed him from an old shrine at Fa'ikwa'u. He describes a man's traditional full dress costume, which is how ancestral ghosts often appear to people. (The *subi* is the short Malaitan club with a lozenge-shaped blade.)

said 'I'm with you'. I was in those pagan districts where my ancestors are, where they still offer sacrifices to the ghosts.

So I went off into the place where all the bamboos were, using a box of matches. But one more strange thing happened. When I came to where the paths met, leaving 'Ere'ere as I went down to Gwa'ifata village, I surprised a man in the night. He stood up above me and said 'Heee'. He was taken by surprise. I was startled and I didn't move because I was so confused, so I just sat down. As I sat a thought came to me, it must have been my mother, saying 'Call out and clear yourself'. Then I remembered what my father had told me long before, that at this place in 'Ere'ere they'd brought a ghost to stay and watch over the place, and if you want to steal and you come in the dark and don't light a bamboo as a torch or carry some fire, he'll kill you. Or if you go into the bush to look for a pig in a certain place and he sees you, you'll die. So if you're there and you want to go somewhere you have to speak to him. So I cried out, like this; 'Eh, don't you know me? I'm a grandson of Nunute'e. I'm a grandson of Bakete. I'm a grandson of Kafisi, I'm a child from here; don't you know me?'[8] Then I took a can of Coca-cola and threw it into the bamboos to make a noise and I shouted and went on, feeling better. Nothing happened and I didn't worry, because I knew my mother was with me and I wasn't afraid because they belonged to me. I belonged to those ghosts and I was one of them.

When I reached home I'd missed everything, but I realised how great were the powers of the ghosts. It's a very important part of our culture. By my own strength alone I can't overcome anything greater than myself, and that's what has

8 These are the names of certain ghosts of the 'Ere'ere clan, from whom Kwa'ioloa is descended on his mother's side. Bakete, a famous warrior, was his mother's father.

kept my ancestors alive until today. As my father told me, those clans who didn't have powerful ghosts all died out long ago, with no-one surviving till today. But I'm sure that those who live on to the present lived by the ghosts, and the ghosts were a powerful thing for my ancestors. I've proved for myself that this thing my fathers and grandfathers lived by in the past is true. But I also want to tell how, while I was still living in Honiara, a year before I got married, a strange thing happened to the country. That was Revival, when the spirit of God was revealed and everyone was filled with it and it changed our religious life.

I'll explain how Revival reached here. In the past our religious services weren't very emotional and our feelings were just as normal. Even when the missionaries used to come and teach us how to organise our church programmes, whenever we held a church service we were the same as normal. That was until 1970, when a preacher from New Zealand called Muri Thompson came to Honiara. He held big meetings in Honiara Central Church. Everyone came and when he preached his preaching really convicted[9] the lives of the people, making them cry and confess their faults, because his preaching really made them feel guilty. If I'd done anything wrong, when the word of God in the Bible came I'd feel guilty. So when he appealed to people to come to the altar, anyone who'd done wrong in any way touched on by the word of God would respond and come to the front. Hundreds of people with tears in their eyes cried and went to the front and he prayed for them. Then something else would happen; they'd be overcome with emotion, they'd cry, people repented their sins, they'd pray over them, pray for blessing and pray to cast

9 When a person 'convicts', as Kwara'ae say in English (*ta'elia* in Kwara'ae), it means an experience of spiritual inspiration when the Holy Spirit or a ghost 'arises in him'.

out demons and for healing. It was the first time this had happened. These things had not been usual or common in the SSEC church since the time I was small.[10]

At the time I didn't believe it either, because I thought I was an educated man. My brother John Maesatana and his family said they believed it, they got into it, experienced it and threw out all their old ways for the sake of Jesus, to live a perfect life. They used to come back and talk to me, but I said 'You lot don't know anything'. Then I fell out with my brother's family even more. Once when my little sister Arana came by she said 'Eh, you don't go to church Michael, and you don't love our big brother. You know he's done lots of things for you, bought you a radio, bought you a camera and built you a house, but you only do what those useless boys tell you. What kind of person are you?' So I got cross and punched her and threw her under a log. That was Satan's doing. Afterwards I was sorry for my sister and I gave her five dollars to make her forget it and love me again, restoring our relationship. She said 'You don't care about our Master, Jesus, that's why you did that to me. But it's all right now.'

At the time me and my uncle Kwasi were living in our own house a few yards from my brother's house. We'd just rush in when it was time to have a meal and then rush out again, because they'd pray in the house. My uncle had been in Fiji for two years at medical school to gain his diploma as a dental mechanic. When he returned from Fiji he gave me lots of things to wear; long trousers, jackets, shoes and these things really made me fond of this man Kwasi. Then a team from Fulisango in West Kwara'ae came over to Honiara and they were holding public services. Daniel Toto was the man.

10 Kwara'ae has a tradition of Christian spiritual 'revival' reaching back to the early days of the South Sea Evangelical Mission, but a mass movement of spirit possession had never happened on this scale before.

When they got there they held a meeting and in the evening Daniel Toto talked to me about things to do with the Master, Jesus.

That night when I went home he prayed for me and went away, and when I went to bed I couldn't sleep. I studied and read, wanting to sleep, and then suddenly I saw a fire come down from the sky and burn my house. That's what changed me. I was a man who didn't believe anyone and I didn't believe in the church or even in God. It burnt my house, but the strange thing was that it only burnt my room and not my uncle's room. So I got up and went to wake my uncle and he swore at me. But I didn't want any swearing, although at that time I used to swear and say all kinds of things. You know how I was living, I don't need to say more. So I didn't swear back. But something was wrong that night and I was still troubled. I woke up a second time after I lay down and I saw the same thing happen again, the fire burning my house. Then the third time I saw my brothers standing at their house and pointing at me and saying 'We've told you already; if you disobey like this you'll die.' That really made me worry that night and I ran off along the path to make myself forget it. And although I didn't need to relieve myself I wanted to, because my belly was very nervous and felt bad. I tried to relieve myself but I couldn't. I went along the path but that was difficult too. I felt bad, crying and nervous, and at the same time the sky became troubled with lightning flashes and thunder. I said 'Eh, maybe this is what they said about Jesus coming back. If he comes back I'll be lost, through my sins.' That made me feel worse. I went home but I didn't sleep.

I stayed awake until dawn and I ran to the church. I told my uncle 'I'm giving up this life of ours' and my uncle said 'If you give it up today you can bring back all the things I've given you today too. That means you and me won't be sharing a cigarette together, we won't be sharing a can of beer, it's all over. When you go to church service you'll be leaving me. We'll split up. So all our things have to come back.' I thought hard but I couldn't give in. After three or four hours I was indeed transformed into a new man. So I ran off to the church and while I was still hidden from sight behind the hibiscus bushes the preacher in the church called out my name. He couldn't yet see me, but the spirit of God had already revealed me to him: 'Michael, Michael.' Then I was frightened again and I didn't come forward because I thought 'Eh, how could he see me? I've come to the church hidden from sight and he hasn't seen me. How could he see me?' Then he said I was troubled because God had already seen me, and that troubled me more. So then I quickly went into the church, crying and crying. The man just held me and I fell to my knees saying 'I'm surrendering my life to Jesus. I want to finish with my old ways.' So when he'd prayed for me and I was feeling all right he dealt with my life and I told him the same things I've told here; everything about me to do with ghosts and dances and everything like that. I've given everything to Jesus now and just told the story of it here. When I'd given out everything they prayed over me to cast out the demon, and for healing and the filling of the Holy Spirit.

All these things left me a long time ago now. If I was to talk about this when it hadn't left me I'd feel strange because I'd be invoking it again. But not now, because Jesus is with me. I accepted Jesus in October 1972. That was when everything I've told about fell away and I knew I had blessing and happiness, and when I went back to the house I returned singing with joy. When I reached my uncle he'd taken all his things back from me, but when I compared material and spiritual things the spiritual ones were more important. So from that time, although I was working for the Express Building Company, starting to build the General Post Office in Honiara, I was in that marvellous life, knowing the presence of Jesus was with me. I knew my life had changed completely from what it was before, with no more fighting and bad things like that. But the blessing remained because Jesus had changed my life and made it peaceful. I no longer joined the people going around town for enjoyment. I didn't get into trouble drinking until ten o'clock, joining the boys to dance in the clubs or joining Rocky Tisa singing worldly songs, as Rocky still does today. True, they'd see me and I wouldn't reject them. I'd talk with them and say 'Oh, I'm taking a rest from all that, because my brother has spoken to me and Jesus has spoken to me. I'm training for the church now.' They all tried hard to pull me back but I wouldn't go. I'd come to the Master.

I just trained for three months or six months, and I was surprised when they said 'Michael, you're going to join the teachers at Sunday School.' I didn't know what I was going to teach. There were evangelical books for children and as I could read I just ran a programme. I got on all right but I still didn't know the word of God. So God led me to ask for two weeks leave from work. Then I studied the word of God until he told me to fast, so I didn't eat and just studied, praying hard for God to lead me so that when I read the Bible I'd understand what the Bible was. Because I was reading it as if it was just a newspaper. When I went to take a service I had to ask an old man to interpret and explain it for me, because the Bible is holy and I knew it was true.[11]

So eventually, after seven days of fasting, the spirit of God led me to Mount Austen where I prayed privately with God until, after he'd tried me with many temptations during one or two hours of prayer, this is what I saw. I was standing in a

11 'Holy' for Kwara'ae means tabu (Kwara'ae *ābu*), and Kwa'ioloa treated the Bible as if it was too sacrosanct for him to interpret by himself. By 'true' he means that it is effective and powerful (Kwara'ae *mamana*).

bright light and there was a pool with nice lilies on it, but I was lifted up from the earth to somewhere else, I don't know where. A man was standing behind me and he said 'Look.' He pointed and I looked. The man was in white linen, and as I looked I saw a white duck go into the pool. It kept on coming until it got close and the man said 'Michael, step down and go down on your knees.' Then I stepped down to the bank of the pool and went down on my knees and the white duck came even closer. The man said 'Put both your hands underneath the duck, in the water.' When I put out my hands the duck laid a white egg and when I took my hands back there was the egg. The duck went back and disappeared among the lilies in that nice quiet pool. Then the man said to me 'Hold the egg in one hand, then break it with the other hand and quickly join your hands together.' So I knelt down and held the egg in my left hand, broke it with my right hand, joined my hands together, and there was the Holy Bible in my hands. That was a great surprise. So then the man said 'That's what you need,' and I said, 'Yes, that is what I need.' With that I suddenly realised what was happening and I said 'But I'm on Mount Austen!' It was dark and I could see by my watch it was seven o'clock. Then I just walked along the path saying 'What am I doing here? I should have stayed there beside the pool', because the pool was such a nice place to be.

So when I returned God led me by His Spirit and I studied the Word of God and surpassed those who'd been to Bible college. It was God who gave me my skill in the ministry of his word. I know this was because God took the person I'd been and changed my spiritual appearance, and I received my gift because I'd fasted and prayed for it and wanted it so much. So then I asked three of my brothers, Hamuel Fa'akaisia, who was a member of the church at Kobito and a former pastor, Nemuel Oto, a man who had been backsliding, and John Osite'e, who was also one of my church members. The Spirit showed me that we should go round all the local churches in Honiara, so I took another three weeks leave without pay. I knew that the Master was leading me when more than a hundred people repented and accepted Jesus through our preaching in the Honiara District Church Association[12], and that made me go deeper into the work of the church.

From then on I knew that the Master had chosen me to do his work, and after that they said 'Now you can be a deacon.' Although I was only a young boy I became a deacon in the church at Kobito One, when we had a single church for the Fataleka and Kwara'ae people.[13] So I knew I was quite mature and doing well in life. While I was a deacon they said 'Michael, you can be our church secretary, to write all our records,' because I had a bit of education. So I held three jobs; Sunday School teacher, deacon and secretary. I enjoyed that a lot. Then as I went ahead and they saw I was doing well they said 'Michael, you and Hamuel can take reading classes every evening.' As I was busy with this work I forgot worldly things like drinking and I was quite satisfied. God guided me so I was too busy to join the others around town, and that's how my life came to be.

12   A District Church Association is the South Sea Evangelical Church organisation uniting the Local Churches, each of which comprises several villages who together elect their own committee and pastor.

13   Fataleka is the language group immediately to the north of Kwara'ae, and as fellow Malaitans they and others like the Kwaio live in some of the same areas around Honiara.

5 *Getting Married*

All this happened after I left school at Betikama, during 1971 and 1972. The time when I lived as a delinquent was only two years and the Master soon cut me free and brought me to this new way which changed my life. While I was leading this Christian life, knowing I'd been saved, I kept my money because I didn't drink beer, I didn't smoke, didn't dance and didn't go to the movies and spend any money. So at the end of the month there wasn't anything to pay, except clothes and a bit of support for the family, and I saved up a bit of money. While I was saving, during the Easter holiday in 1973, my brother and sister-in-law went on holiday to Fulisango in Malaita and I stayed in Honiara.

Now in our tradition if my brother alone is married with no-one to help him, even if I was a young boy he'd tell me I had to get married so I could also help some of our people, because he was only one man. Just imagine if all of us from East Kwara'ae came to stay in his house and there was only him. When I was young we had twenty-five to thirty plates at one meal. We weren't short of food because all of them helped make a big garden, so that was all right. But my brother Maesatana still said 'Father, I want to make Michael get married. Even though he's only a boy I want him to marry and follow our tradition.' That was when I was twenty one. So while he was away the two of them discussed it in secret and I didn't know. Then he went to see a girl at Fulisango, a girl whose father had died, and he watched how she behaved. She looked as if she was modest and good in church matters. He asked everyone there about her background and she wasn't the kind of girl who'd misbehaved when she was young. So he asked for her.

With us, in our tradition, the first thing they look for in a girl when they approach her family is her work. She has to be a worker, not a lazy girl. Because in the past it was the girls who fed the pigs, who cooked food for the pigs and the people, it was the girls who went to the gardens to do the weeding and everything, who filled the bamboo bottles with drinking water and cut the firewood. That was in the past, and that's why we had to look for a girl who'd work. And secondly, a girl had to be kind to her people. It was no good taking a girl who chased everyone away and didn't want anyone to visit. Thirdly, she had to be a girl who didn't rush into things or shout at anyone in the family. She had to be a quiet girl. And as far as the church is concerned, nowadays a girl must accept Jesus as her saviour and be concerned for the Master. She'll join church activities such as the women's band, the singing band and Sunday school. She'll become a member of the church, not to hold the services but to sweep the church, decorate the church and help to prepare food when visitors come.[1]   And my brother saw all this in my wife.

So he asked for her from her grandfather Haman Namusia, an old man of Fulisango village in West Kwara'ae. He asked for my wife and all her brothers approved and said 'That's all right.' But the girl also wanted to see; 'Oh, first let me see if this boy's smart and if I like him or not.' Then my brother came back and asked me to go with him for the girl to see. That made me really embarrassed and I said 'Eh, how will I appear when this girl sees me? She might be a really nice pretty girl, and I'll be just rubbish.'

But you know, when I was a young man I didn't look good when I dressed myself up. It was like this; I'll describe it. I had long hair when I was young and I usually wore sunglasses and I always wore bellbottoms and I really liked the kind of

---

1   In the SSEC, 'members' are fully qualified participants in the church, who join in conducting church services if they are men but have less prestigious duties if they are women.

shirt that had cords across the chest. Sometimes I'd double up with both a teeshirt and a jacket. With all this I'd wear a wristwatch and I liked to carry a camera and use perfumes. I adopted European culture, because I'd been to school and seen all these things. When I was born again I dressed up even more to go to service. But before that when I dressed up I'd have a long cigarette in my mouth so I'd smell bad, like when I was dancing and I burnt the breast of the Fijian woman and she chased me off. It was things like that which made me reflect and say 'No, I think I'll change my life.'

But at that time I'd planned to spend another five or ten years of my life going to Bible college at Onepusu,[2] earning more money and preaching for a while, so I'd reach the age of thirty before I got married. But what my brother told me was 'You've seen these five red shell moneys for yourself; if you disobey me and don't want to marry this girl and want to marry a different one, it's up to you. But if any other brothers get married I'll give all the money away to pay for them. Because you're not thinking according to tradition. Father has spoken to me and you know that what the important men want is best. What you choose for yourself is no good.' I had no mother or any other brother to help me besides John Maesatana, who was like my own father. My father was still living in Malaita, staying with Patrick Nunute'e, with Authaban Maniramo and Sango'iburi, following our old way of life and supported by John Maesatana in Honiara.

At the same time I'd made friends with another girl, at home near our village. But when my father went to ask for her from her brother he almost attacked my father with a knife. So when I heard I said 'No, I don't want her. Let that girl go.' So now I was willing; 'Oh, that's fine.' Then my brother said 'Okay, we'll buy some things to take so you can

2 The SSEC training college on the south-west coast of Malaita.

give them for the engagement.' The two of us bought ten
fathoms of cloth, special linen, and then got some more
money to buy a finger ring with a chain, and off we went. We
reached 'Aoke and went up into the bush and I thought hard
and said 'How am I going to look when the girls come to see
me?' because I was really embarrassed. I was only willing to
make the engagement because my brother John Maesatana
said 'You have to go and make this engagement.[3] If she's
going to do nothing but look at you we might as well not go.'

So that Sunday afternoon everyone returned from service
and they all knew I'd be coming that day. When we came out
into the village I was really scared because they'd all gathered
together in the house of old man Namusia. I was carrying my
radio and my camera and the first house we came to, although
I didn't know the house, I just went inside. Even though I
hadn't asked the man of the house I went in because they
were all waiting over there. So I sat on the veranda, put my
radio on the table, and my camera, and waited while my
brother went on to the house and they talked. 'Has Kwa'i
come?' 'Yes, he's there; Michael's over there.' So all the
women came with a man called Saukwai who was the girl's
uncle. They all came in and shook my hand and I didn't know
which one was my wife. But my wife was among them. Then
I had a strange feeling as if I was fenced in so that my life
couldn't widen out, but because I'd accepted Jesus my life was
happy. So then they revealed who she was, and the girl's
uncle said 'Okay, come and shake hands with the one you're
going to pay for.' So with that the girl just looked at me and
her uncle asked 'Do you like him?' My wife said 'Oh yes, I
like him now I've seen him', and she did like me. And then he
asked me, 'So, do you like her?' I said 'I'm not saying I like

3 'Engaging' to be married (*alu fafia*) involves a presentation of goods which
is in effect a deposit towards the bridewealth gift (*daura'ia*).

her and I'm not saying I don't like her. The answer depends on my brother, because he asked for her. If he says yes, I'll accept her. If he says no, then no it is.' That was because my brother had already accepted her. It was he who asked for her, so the answer was 'Yes', not from me but from my brother.

So that Sunday evening we went to service and I carried the parcel of clothes, with the finger ring and skirts and things, according to the way of the church, and I went up when they were to pray over the two of us and just gave them. It was the first time I'd given clothes to this girl and when I did it my life changed again; 'Eh, I'm going to be married!' I thought hard, because the thing was, I didn't want to marry. I'd lived with my brother and seen the married way of life. He had children, he was busy, there was salt to buy, kerosene to buy, soap to buy. I bought all this too, but only enough for myself, but everything depended on him and he had to buy the food. That's why I didn't want to marry too soon. But now my life had changed, because I'd given that parcel. The church minister announced that 'From now onwards this girl belongs to this boy, Michael. Bizel Fane belongs to him. So now Michael is engaged.'

So at the time of the engagement, after dark when we came back, Bizel brought her bed for me to sleep on, and from that time she'd always do my washing. I didn't touch her, because she was like a sister. Then after I'd stayed there for two weeks during the Christmas holiday my brother Maesatana and I went back, and when we went he said the marriage had to wait until November. What happened next was that Fane's elder brother almost stopped it. Then the girl thought about all the things I'd given her and when they asked them to carry some bags of food down to 'Aoke to send to her uncle Maeka who worked in the police force, she knew they were going to stop her so she refused to carry the bag. They asked her what it was, she told them and they beat her and her brother punched her. Her brother was angry and he asked his uncle John Daota, who went straight to Honiara.

He arrived one night and gave us a shock, saying 'Bring five red shell moneys John Maesatana, for my nephew to receive for your brother.' So that night about nine o'clock my cousin Fa'akaisia and John Maesatana went to wake my sister Helen Misani in their house to check for a key to the box. It was one of those old wooden boxes with a bell that rang; 'Eh, the box is ringing!' Everyone was startled but it was only them taking out the five red shell moneys. They washed them in Omo, dried them, and early in the morning my father-in-law Daota took them and went back.

The five red shell moneys came from my brother John Maesatana and myself. That wasn't quite right according to our tradition, what John Maesatana did, because we should have been helping one another. John Maesatana should have said 'Brothers, our little brother is getting married. I'm going to pay for her on such and such a day.' If he'd done that something like ten or twenty red shell moneys would have come. But John Maesatana didn't want that. Maybe because he'd left us long before he was thinking 'I can pay it all myself.' I realised this because the next day my fathers started speaking out. They said 'What's all this? The man's already paid it! Hey, why didn't you say? There's a shell money here!' So they tried to contribute hundreds of dollars for the feast, but Maesatana stopped that too. He said 'No, I've got enough. Otherwise I'm going to be too much in debt.' He'd put a limit on it, exchanged some things, fed a pig which they bought for a red shell money, and when one of our sisters, Asu, got married we received a *bani 'au* shell money. Another one came from Bualimae's daughter living in Honiara, my daughter Kibora; when she got married I received another *bani 'au*. So we put it all together and Maesatana said 'That's enough.' It wasn't quite right to do it this way but it was good for us because if we'd received too much shell money, when other marriages came up my money would be gone and if my own sons didn't have shell money we'd be out of luck. That's why it was all right. So my brother brought all five of the red shell moneys and gave them all at once, and my father-in-law went off back to Malaita.[4]

I'd wanted the feast to wait, thinking 'Oh, that's all right, in November we'll do everything at once.' But my wife wanted it sooner, maybe because she'd heard more rumours that the family were going to break the engagement. So she may have rushed it, and they said September 8th. When I came back to prepare the feast my brother and me spent more money, especially me. We bought five pigs and we performed a big feat by starting in the east and carrying them on our shoulders to the west, through the central bush where there was still no proper road. One pig was worth two red shell moneys, and we carried it on a litter until we were tired, and then led it on a rope. This feast was so big that one man and his brother couldn't have done it alone. Just imagine walking about ten miles carrying pigs on your shoulders. Five pigs is a lot of work. On one day we took the four smaller ones and left them at Fi'ika'o at Osifera's place, and then another day everyone just moved the very big one. Then me and Maesatana bought some food from Osifera's village and we carried it the short distance to Fulisango. At the same time I'd bought food at 'Afi'o by previous arrangement and that's why

---

4 In fact the five red shell moneys given was the amount of bridewealth set by the churches. Kwa'ioloa is describing pressures from his relatives to follow traditional practices of negotiating larger quantities of bridewealth, which would have obligated him and his family to repay large contributions from others over a period of many years, or even into the next generation. *Bani 'au* is a large shell money denomination, equivalent in value to the ten-string *tafuli 'ae* but deriving from the shell money system of Kwaio.

everything worked out well. When we reached Fulisango it was night and everyone was really tired.

So we celebrated the marriage feast on September 8th 1973, and it was then my life changed from that of a young man to a married man. Well, I knew something about weddings and I'd seen other people's, but I wasn't sure as I hadn't been through it myself. When I experienced it myself, when we came back and made the arrangements to gather the pigs and firewood, the leaves and oven-stones for the wedding feast, and bought the taro, things were a bit different. The difference was that among us, with a holy marriage in church, the girl's side had to provide five pigs for the red shell moneys they'd received and then my side, the man's, had to provide another five pigs. That's for a church marriage. Then we chose the place and took the garden food there, such as taro and sweet potatoes, and they brought garden food too, taro and sweet potatoes, and we put it all together and made one big feast. But before we did that my brother bought a bag of rice and a carton of tinned fish and left it there with the girl's side, because all the celebrations would be at the place where the girl lived. The reason for leaving the rice and fish there was so that when the man's side were there preparing everything in advance they could eat it. So I began helping with this big project, supporting my wife's family during the celebrations. And whenever they were cutting firewood and doing other work, one or two from my side would join them to prepare things. That meant we were already joining together as one family. Eventually, when everything was ready, on the last day before the feast all the pigs arrived at once and everything came together.[5]

---

5 Kwa'ioloa would like to record his thanks to all his relatives who helped him with his wedding.

Then on that night the girl's preaching band sang with her. They showed their joy with her and she had to sing with them because next day she was going to leave. So it was a big event all night and people didn't sleep. They listened to the singing, enjoying themselves and meeting one another, the man's side meeting the girl's side. It was exciting for people from East and West to gather in the same place and very unusual too. They saw new faces and maybe the boys from one side were looking at the girls from the other side and getting some surprises, all my sisters and my brothers.

For something like this people have to co-operate to make it happen. A man can't do it alone. And this co-operation doesn't come from nowhere, in our tradition. It happens because when you're a young man and someone gets married you're there too, and not for nothing; your shell money and your work goes as well. Then when you do something yourself everyone's with you. That's what I did. When my brothers got married, even though I was in Honiara I contributed shell money. Sometimes, before I was married, I took part in weddings, dressed up and joined the wedding party, the group which accompanies them to the church, some on the girl's side, some on the man's side. They dress up in jackets and long trousers, shoes and things, maybe three girls and three men, and join together until they've prayed over them. So that's what happened when all my brothers gave me their help, and that's how we carried out my marriage safely and happily.

But one thing was different from when I was little, looking back on my life. In the church I had three men with me and we were dressed in expensive clothes which we'd bought; long trousers, boots, ties and things, with shirts and jackets. My brother spent a lot of money on that wedding. We had to get ready in a house and we had all sorts of things such as powders and perfumes to smell nice. He also bought a mat and a new pillow for the two of us to kneel on in the church. And I bought the costumes the women dressed in, very expensive ones, with long dresses reaching the ground. They covered their hair with soft linen as well, expensive too. That's what my wife did too, but she had a special dress which I bought. It's not an easy thing to get married in church.

So when we were all prepared the singing groups came to escort us. One singing group came to escort us men first; they came in four lines and divided to make a space in the middle with two lines on each side. Then we went in between, myself and the girl's brother, who would hold my hand because he was going to give the girl to me. Then for the girl, a brother of mine held onto her too, one who was related to her and to me. So we formed a long row in the church, with a man standing between the two of us because he was going to give the girl to me. When we were standing there they made us give the marriage oath. We had to follow the minister; 'Well, when you live with this girl, will you be true to her? In time of trouble, for richer for poorer, in time of sickness, in good times, until death parts you?' I said 'I do.' I gave the oath before God and before the congregation and before my wife. Then my wife did the same; 'I solemnly declare.' When we'd given the oath they asked the congregation as well and gave them about three minutes, saying 'If anyone wants to prevent this marriage, let him speak now, or else God will bind the two of them together forever.' While we waited I worried a bit and said 'My word, that's one question I could do without,' because I'd already spent all the money for the wedding and the feast. If at the last minute anyone had blocked it, that would have been a serious matter, something I wasn't prepared for. But when they'd been silent for three minutes the minister lifted his head and looked at me and my wife, looked at everyone and said 'Whatsoever God has joined together, let no-one put asunder.'

Well, my life was changing again. I heard and I thought hard; 'I said I'd be true to her, and my wife said she'd be true to me.' Because I'd said even when we were poor, even when we were rich, even when she was sick and ill or threw up over me, I'd be the one to wash her and everything. That was another way of life! But I told myself I'd have to try hard to maintain my promise if ever I was called upon to fulfil it.

One part which was a bit strange was when they said 'Who's giving this girl to this man?' Then one of her brothers, Toto, said 'Me', and I said 'What's this? Okay, come and give her.' When he said that he walked over and said 'Where's the ring?' Then I held the ring and I showed it on my finger, and he took my wife's finger, put them together and pushed the ring from my finger and onto my wife's. And when he held our hands together, the moment I held my wife's hand it brought tears to my eyes. That's when the world changed, because I hadn't touched that girl, my wife, before, and I didn't know who she was. So the moment I touched her and we stood there holding hands, the world changed. I felt like crying and I felt in awe of her. She was the same. We both felt a bit like that and I just stood there without moving. But suddenly they said 'You both kneel down' and all of us knelt down and prayed. They prayed over both of us and united us.

I'll explain a bit more about what happened at the wedding feast. While we were busy in the church the senior men stayed behind and opened up the stone ovens where we were baking the pigs. But before baking them they'd made an exchange. One big pig from the man's side was given to the girl's side and then they gave a big one to the man's side. They exchanged them to settle the marriage. Then the two groups made their separate preparations; the man's side killed their pig themselves and the girl's side killed their pig themselves, and they made two separate ovens to cook them in, with sweet potatoes and taro. Then when they opened up

the ovens the senior men, my fathers, my brother John
Maesatana and the brothers of my wife Bizel Fane, shared out
their own ovens according to who had supported them. They
shared theirs among their village, and for my side my brother
and my father shared among the group who'd come with us.
If I wanted to give some pieces of pork to those on my wife's
side, he'd give it to them too, but we wouldn't make a single
big platform and throw all the pigs onto it and all eat. No, it
wasn't a party. We shared out the food so that each person
who'd made a contribution would receive a bit of pork, and
the sizes of the pieces of pork depended on how the shell
money had come in. It wasn't like paying for it, but if a man
had helped with a red shell money for the marriage, I'd give
him a big piece of pork. Or if a man gave me fifty dollars, the
piece of pork I'd give him would be a large one. If a man gave
me five or ten dollars, I'd give according to the money I'd
received. Then we divided everything until everyone had a
share and everyone ate at the wedding. That's how they did
it for us.

I've already told how the Christian life made me humble,
and married life made me even more humble. So the night I
took my wife into the house it was hard for me to sleep with
her, because she was an unfamiliar girl and I was unfamiliar,
she was frightened and I was a bit frightened too. So that
night in the house I was afraid to sleep with my wife, and I
went outside to see someone else and we talked. But they'd
laid out the bed for me and my wife and that night was my
first time to sleep with a woman. I was thinking how I was
going to sleep with the woman and she was thinking the same
thing. So when they'd laid out the bed and it was time for
everyone to go to their room to sleep, she was in our room.

To explain how I felt about the girl, in Honiara I'd made
friends with some girls in the past, but that was a dishonest

kind of friendship, and I was stealing.[6] And the girls I'd been friends with, I didn't go far with them. The only thing I did was to touch the girl, we'd enjoy ourselves and that was it. The kind of thing you do when you're properly married, anything like that was new to me. So when I came into the room I didn't think my wife would be sleeping there, but there she was. But she wasn't lying on the bed, just sitting at the table. She was asleep, but lying with her head on the table. So when I opened the door I spoke to my wife, 'Hey,' I said, 'Wake up'. My wife looked at me and I could see she was frightened, and I was a bit frightened too. Then I stopped; she didn't speak to me and I didn't speak to her either. The only thing she said was 'Your food's over there, I'll bring it to the table.' So then I ate, but I felt embarrassed about it. I said 'Come on, we'll both eat,' but she said 'I've already eaten.' I said 'Please come, let's both eat.' So she came closer, but not very close because we were both a bit embarrassed; we both ate a little but we didn't even finish the plate of food between us. We only ate a bit because she was embarrassed and so was I, so we just left it.

Then I said 'Oh Bizel, maybe you should close your eyes, I'm just going to pray.' Then I prayed, I thanked God for giving me a wife and I prayed that he'd teach me how to teach her. The first thing that came to my mind was my father and how he'd taught me. So as soon as we'd said 'Amen', I took my butcher's knife and held her and began like a man on the attack. Whether I was attacking or teaching her I don't know, but it was something I felt inspired to do, to teach her. As I held the knife I put it on the table and told my wife 'Hold onto the knife with me, with my hand.' My wife was frightened, but I said 'Please, put your hand on the handle of

---

6 That is, he was taking the girl without the permission of her family, which would only be given for marriage.

the knife.' When we were both holding the knife together I looked her straight in the eyes and said 'Look, stare into my eyes.' She looked until her eyes grew red, and my eyes grew red, and I said 'If I ever see anyone lie on top of you, I'll use this knife to cut your throat.' That's how I spoke to her, and that changed things, because now the girl understood me. So that night I really taught her what I knew in my own heart, that I didn't want anyone else to fall in love with my wife, following my culture.

Then she cried and I prayed again for forgiveness. I said, 'I attacked you, and according to the law that's wrong, but I'm teaching you what I know to be right. However good looking you are, and however well you look after me, the day I find you with a man, making trouble with you and lying on top of you, that day I'll cut your throat, and the man's too.' So any nervous feelings she had about looking down on me were finished at that time and now she was afraid of me. Then we both prayed for forgiveness and shook hands, and after that she wasn't afraid of me and I wasn't afraid of her, and I began to teach her as my father had told me.

It would take too long to detail all the things I told her, but here are a few of them. I said 'It's tabu to swear at me, and if you swear at me or if you're not kind to my brothers or my father, however good and pretty you are, you'll be out. Secondly, if I hear any of my sisters say 'I found your wife with a man in the bush, or at the water place or at the market, talking and playing together alone', however good and pretty you are, you'll go back to your parents and I'll take back my shell money.' That's one warning I gave her. 'You be kind to my family and I'll be kind to your family.' Whatever my father had said I taught her that night, until about two o'clock, and it was late in the night before we went to sleep. Then I touched her and she touched me, and from that time our relationship began.

Then after the marriage, what else was there? We shook hands and said goodbye and then my wife didn't want to leave and wanted to stay longer and cried, and her mothers and fathers were crying too. Because from East to West Kwara'ae is a long way and my wife was thinking what it meant to leave her home. But they said to her 'You're not going to your death! You'll go on living with that family because of your marriage, but you'll be back to see us again.'

Something very special happened to my life at that time, and looking right back from the day my mother bore me until then I thought I'd taken a very important step on my way through life, and now I was on the last stage. Because I knew that marriage wasn't just something to be tried out and then changed. It's 'Until death parts us'. And the more I experienced married life, bringing up my children and developing relationships with my brothers and sisters, the more I realised what a good thing marriage was. It quietened me down and helped me as a Christian and people recognised me as an adult man and an important person. Once I was married I became respected by people and respected as important in the church, and then they ordained me as a pastor.

6 *Home to Malaita, Family and Work*

After I got married, on the 8th of September 1973, I went back to live in Honiara, then I gave in my notice to the company I was working for and me and my wife boarded the *Compass Rose II* and returned to Malaita.[1] Certain thoughts made me come back. I now knew all about town life and I was interested in it, but because I'd turned to religion my mind was no longer really open to town interests. When I thought about it, town life seemed difficult because it cost money. That's why I said 'I'd better go back home.' And besides, I wanted to help my father, because he was an old man and our tradition says that if I don't help my father it's as if I'm just an irresponsible boy. So this made me think hard, because whenever I'd misbehaved before they told my father and it really broke his heart. I knew I was guilty but I misbehaved because my body wanted pleasure; my blood wanted it. But this kind of thinking had stopped because I reconsidered everything when I took up the Christian life, and I knew that my father was more important. And when I compared traditional life and Christian life, the two were much the same. Only the pagan offerings of pig sacrifice are a bit different, but cultural things are the same as for the church, and there's tabu in the church too.[2] That's what made me come back.

When I came back to live at home I had four hundred dollars on deposit in the bank, in my passbook. At the time I thought that was quite enough, because I was comparing it with life at home in the past, when I had no money. When I

---

1 One of the ships making scheduled journeys around Solomon Islands.

2 That is to say, Kwara'ae Christianity identifies holiness as equivalent to the traditional concept of tabu (*ābu*).

had four hundred dollars I said 'Oh, when I'm living at home I'll really be a man with money to live on!' But not quite!

When I reached home I went to live with my brother Maniramo, and in the first week I built myself a new house. I extended his house and put three rooms onto it, two bedrooms and a living or dining room, and I lived there while I was deciding to make my own big house. Then I settled at the place where Ben came to visit me, Anobala. I thought I'd make Anobala separate from the place my uncles were living, Nunute'e and the others. I wanted to live by the river, where it would be easy for my wife to carry drinking water, wash the plates and saucepans and bring water for cooking; you know, water is essential for life. That's why, even though I felt bad leaving my uncle and sisters and brothers there, I had to move. Then one of my fathers, Jephat I'ana, accompanied me and we both lived at Anobala.

While I was living at Anobala I followed the lifestyle of my traditional culture. I didn't make gardens while I was living in Honiara but when I lived at Anobala I bought an axe, a bush-knife, a brushing knife and things like that. I realised that married life was going to be rather difficult for me, because everything depended on me. While I was a young man it wasn't hard because I just bought my own clothes and bedding and that was all. I used to support my brother, but only a little. But now I realised that married life was more difficult. When the salt was finished, I had to pay for it, when the kerosene was finished, I had to pay for it, when we were feeling hungry, I had to work, and if I was lazy I didn't eat. When I thought of cooking food in a good saucepan, I had to buy it. It cost money, and that's what made it hard.

And then as time went on it got harder still. Before I'd been a good-looking boy, interested in using perfumes and scented things and bathing with soap, and I used to iron my clothes a bit before I put them on, and have other nice things.

But when I married this woman and we were living together, within a year's time we had a child. So from that time it got even more difficult, because it was me who had to carry the child. Before I didn't used to carry children, and when I carried my child he'd pee on me and it started to spoil my clothes. Sometimes I got cross and said 'Eh, this child's peeing on me, on my best clothes.' Then my wife said 'You're not a young man any more, you're a married man and you'll have to live like a married man. You're not a young man; are you trying to do yourself up to get another girl? We're married now. I don't like it either, but I've borne a child and you and me have to carry him and he's going to shit on us and pee on us and throw up on us'. That's what she told me. So then the easiest thing for me to do was to accept that I had to look after the child well and leave the young men. If I went around with the young men I wouldn't be helping my wife, so I told them 'Sorry brothers, I can invite you to eat but I can't go with you and stay the night in some other house, or go to talk about things in another village or go and play the guitar with you somewhere else, or go to Honiara whenever we want. That's finished, because now I've got a wife and child.'

So I realised my life was becoming divided. When I took my wife my love for her really affected me, because now there were two of us. But when I had my firstborn son, my love for myself decreased even more and became, you might say, secondary. At first everything had been for myself, then there was my wife who I bought clothes and everything for, and that meant a decrease in my love for myself. Then, when there was the child too, I really was secondary. When I compared myself with when I was a young single boy, I had to be humble. Those were the thoughts that came to me, and what's more they were my father's ideas, and I realised that what he'd told me was bound to happen. I had to become a family man and no longer behave as if I could just please

Timi Ko'oliu, last senior priest of 'Ere'ere and Kwara'ae, father of Kwa'ioloa's brother-in-law Le'a (1979).

Siubata, wife of
Timi Ko'oliu, and
their daughter
Musuba'eko,
wearing the
traditional costume
of married women,
a fibre and bead
belt and apron.
(1979)

Le'akini, daughter
of Timi Ko'oliu
(actually his
brother's daughter),
with young friends a
few years before her
marriage, which
Kwa'ioloa attended
in Kwaio. She wears
a red fibre belt, the
traditional costume
of an unmarried girl.
(1979)

Sharing out a bridewealth presentation in 'Ere'ere in 1984. On the right is Kwa'ioloa's brother-in-law Le'a, son of Timi Ko'oliu.

Kwa'ioloa as pastor for Mamulele Church, leading their singing band
at the opening of a new church at the Kobito suburb of Honiara, in
1977. (photographer unknown)

Working for the ATASI sawmill at Gwarimudu, in 1984.

myself. So when I lived as a married man, within about two years I had another child, and with the second child I realised that I was really being brought down, and the further down I went the more I matured in traditional ways, and obeyed our rules.

In the past, as I watched my brother John Maesatana when his children were very naughty, I thought if that child was mine I'd smack him or even beat him because he was so naughty. When I had children myself I tried hard to do that but eventually I became quite humble. Because when the child behaved like that I thought how many times I'd have to beat him. It might be hundreds of times I'd have to beat the child and I might even kill him. So I said 'Oh, I give up. I'll have to be humble in looking after my children, because I hope to have maybe three or four or five or six or maybe even seven children.' So the more humble I became, the quieter I was and my temper was more controlled, because I had been a man who got angry very quickly. When I took up spiritual and religious things and became a church leader I grew humble and good-tempered, because Jesus quietened me down and because my children made me really humble too. That's what children do.

I wanted many children because my father told me 'You must have lots of children because our clan is disappearing. I'm the one man who fathered you all.' That's the reason, because we've got lots of ways to prevent children and they're born according to our wishes, but my father said that shouldn't happen. 'You must have lots of children, to take my place and raise up our clan of Tolinga, Fi'ika'o and Fairū.' I also wanted lots of children because I've got lots of land and there's no development in it yet, and all us brothers related to this land will have children to develop it. And when I have lots of children people respect me, because I'm well established with people to help me to work and assist other families.[3] That's why I have so many children, and I'm quite proud of them all and how we all love each other. I'm always affectionate to my children and even with my firstborn son Lawrence Lau, I still hug him sometimes when I'm pleased with his work. And I'm pleased that they obey me and live quietly without bothering other people's families or getting involved with girls, and they're religious too.

I'm lucky enough to have ten children, and one after another me and my wife have really loved and cared for them. My first child, Lawrence Laugere, was born in 1974 and my father named him after my grandfather Laugere. Then I've had another every two years for twenty-one years until now I have ten. Wilson Maelua was the next, named after my ancestor who had nearly ten children, and increased us to the numbers we are today. I'm not like some families where they just think up a name; the names in my family had to be approved by my father. My third son, Hamilton Namusia, was named after my wife's grandfather at Fulisango. He was an important man there, a chief, who died after we got married. Another son is Joses Lilifafia, named after his uncle, my wife's brother. Another boy is called Michael Maeisua. Maeisua was an important ancestor of mine whose daughter Bingamae was given a lot of land because they'd killed him. The land was given as death-compensation because she cried to her brothers about what they'd done and they said 'We won't give pigs or shell money, but we'll hand over the pieces of land which led to your father's death.' Another of my children is called Alden Afutana. Afutana was the real name

3 Kwa'ioloa's pride in a large family is common in Kwara'ae, where only a generation ago many children died in infancy (like half of his own brothers and sisters). Although the population of Malaita and Solomon Islands is multiplying rapidly, Kwa'ioloa argues that his family have large areas of unoccupied land and a modest standard of living which does not consume too much resources.

of my father; Alasa'a was a nickname. Then I started to have girls. The first was Annie Maranabua. Maranabua was my mother's mother, married to Bakete. The second was Pauline Lekafa'iramo. Lekafa'iramo was my father's mother and Pauline is after Ben Burt's wife whom he brought to visit us in Solomon Islands. Another is Rosie Ro'i junior, named after my wife's mother. The last one is named after Ben Burt. I couldn't do this without approval and it's a big thing to interrupt my lineage with a name from England, so I asked my father Peter Finia back home. I called him Ben Burt junior so that when the Kwara'ae call his name they'll think of Ben, who helped them by writing everything down for us, and because he's helped my family as a brother. That's my last child; I won't have any more.

While I was living at Anobala something else happened; this man Le'a came to take my sister Sango'iburi. Le'a is the son of Timi Ko'oliu, the last senior priest of 'Ere'ere, so she married the son of another senior priest, in 1975. Le'a came round one day to where the garden was and he asked my sister, but she didn't want him. She said 'What, a pagan man like you? Who's going to want you?' What next? He made some of their traditional magic and came round again, met Sango'iburi beside the garden and asked her again. Then this thing got to her and she packed up and off they went. So I went after him, received five red shell moneys, made a bit of a feast to celebrate the marriage, and she went to live with them up the hill in 'Ere'ere at a place called Gwa'ibaola.

Sango'iburi became a pagan and she had to feed pigs for sacrifices to the ghosts, and every day she lived for the ghosts. If there was sickness or anything like that, they had to offer a pig to the ghosts for a cure. If they needed blessings they had to offer a pig to a ghost to safeguard them or bring blessing on the garden or make people help them by giving them shell money or food and things. It didn't come from nowhere; it happened because they asked the ghosts to do it for them. That's why she had to feed pigs, because life came from pigs, blessings came from pigs and whatever they needed came from pigs. If they wanted to fight someone, they'd ask the ghost with a pig; he'd give you strength and safeguard you until you'd achieved what you wanted. So she came to be pagan and feed pigs for the second time. She dressed like a pagan woman and they only let her wear clothes when she went to market or visited us, and then she just put on a skirt. That's how she lived for the ghosts.

While we were living in Malaita, me and my wife took good care of my father and I was kind to her people, and she'd take me on the walk many miles back to her parents' place. Every few months we'd carry fish to her fathers and brothers and sisters at Fulisango, and they'd help us with clothing and things like that. Because of the way I was living at home I soon used up the four hundred dollars; it only lasted a year and when it was finished things were a bit difficult.

And I had some bad luck too. Soon after we moved home me and my wife went to wash our clothes in the river, and we didn't expect the river to flood. We put all our things to dry out in a place where there was some dry gravel and we thought we'd have a picnic, so me and one of my brothers, Idufera, went to cook a pig. We took out its guts, cut up the meat and started to enjoy it, and my wife came to start a fire to make the stone oven. But suddenly the water came up and covered the whole area where our clothes were. The bedsheets and everything I'd bought and all our belongings which we'd taken there for the meal were lost at that moment. The dishes and everything were lost. I was really upset about that, because I had no money, I had no clothes; everything was lost. That made me very worried and as I thought about it the situation seemed more and more difficult. My wife had only five pieces of cloth. I said to her, 'You can't hide your breasts now mother; you'll have to go naked like a traditional girl of the past, or just wear an apron in front. We'll go back to paganism.' I joked about it, and my wife had a good laugh.

We decided to buy some more clothes when the Province gave me a job as District Clerk, for Faumamanu District.[4] After Ramofunu finished they took me on, and the work I did for the Province helped me a lot as far as money was concerned. I received an allowance for the days they were sitting of six dollars a day, so I was quite lucky. I had to try to increase the days I worked to be working full time, so I went on to register people for the elections, and as a rate collector I worked to collect taxes in the constituency. While doing that I exempted the old people who weren't able to pay tax and wrote letters of recommendation to the doctor so he'd stop them having to pay, because their children were paying tax. That was my job. At that time the tax was four dollars a year. At the same time I sometimes recorded court cases as Court Clerk too. That was my work, to deal with the Malaita Council for my District.

Then they told us 'Form an Area Committee,' and this was going on while I was working for the District. The Malaita Council at 'Aoke was for Malaita as a whole, and they set up this system of Area Committees for the districts. The members came from the different clans and they were skilful speakers who also had to know about development and about everybody's needs and political concerns in the District. They had to make sure that the clinics were working well and had what they needed and contact the Malaita Council to deal with things like that. For example; 'We want a water supply here at Faumamanu.' If you were just one man asking the

---

4   That is, he was appointed by the Malaita Council (later Malaita Province) as Clerk for East Kwara'ae, the area formerly known as Kwai District, which had its headquarters at the coastal marketplace of Faumamanu (later relocated to 'Atori).

Malaita Council for that, they wouldn't take you seriously. The people's needs must first be taken to the Area Committee, the Area Committee would discuss and investigate it, and when they were sure it was reasonable and helpful to the people of that village or community, they'd approve it and forward it to the Malaita Council, which would allocate money for it or apply for it to the national government. That was the work of the Area Committee.

When the Area Committee was set up we just started it in the market-place at Faumamanu with a few people. We selected Stephen Oge Sande as our Chairman and, as Members, David Suda of A'arai, David Timi of Nazareth, Bualimae of Fa'ibeabea, Sokemae of Nāfinua, Justus Ofo'imae of Gwa'i'ai, Armuel Fangamae of Faumamanu Tolo and Jack Amasia of Ngongosila island. Jeremel Le'anafaka was our Messenger and I was our Clerk. The work of these leaders was to meet and discuss anything of importance and the men we selected were chiefs, the 'important men' of the clans.[5] They were men who had previously worked for the Council, or for the Agriculture department, or for tradition. I was Clerk because they knew I had some idea of how to record things; not very much, but I could keep everything in order.

An important man is someone everyone in the clan relies on. He's a man who can explain the genealogies, a man who knows all about tabu, a man who can organise people to do things, who can stop fighting, who everyone obeys if he speaks, who can make big feasts, and this important man is the one person everyone respects and looks up to. So it was all the important men who came together for the Committee, and the agenda we set was taken from the thoughts of people

5 Kwara'ae often call local leaders *ngwae 'inoto 'a*, 'important man', or *ngwae lalifu*, 'deep-rooted man'; in Pijin or English they are 'bigmen', as in other Melanesian societies. 'Chief' more or less translates *gwaunga'i ngwae*, 'headman' or 'elder'.

outside, and the problems or difficulties to be solved by the Province. That's how we established the Area Committee, which is now the Area Council, and during the same period I also established a committee of chiefs, approved by the national and Malaita governments, which they called the Traditional Chiefs' Sub-Committee.[6]

Although I was Secretary for the Area Council in the East, I often had to go over to the West too, and our meeting place there was the headquarters at 'Aimela. The first time we met there, the two sides of Kwara'ae, West and East, they thought we should make one single Committee. We started that in 1978, and when we began to choose who should be our Secretary the Deputy Clerk of the Malaita Council was keeping the records. They wanted a man specifically to do that job and all the secretaries came along, but they may have been afraid to take the job because when we were all in the building at 'Aimela there were more than a hundred people. When they took fright Sardias Oge, Chairman of the newly established East Kwara'ae Area Committee, seemed to think I'd be able to handle the job. As time passed and no-one was willing, he said 'Oh, perhaps my Secretary Michael Kwa'ioloa should try it. If he does the work properly he can carry on, but if he doesn't really understand things we'll give the job to someone else, or give it to the Deputy Clerk of the Council to do permanently.'

So I was chosen again, and that same day I sat down with a record book which the Council gave me and recorded at the same time as the Deputy Clerk. We made separate records and after the meeting ended at twelve o'clock they took them

6 Organisations of 'traditional' (*kastom* or customary) chiefs, which Kwa'ioloa has also been involved with, were set up by Kwara'ae activists in parallel with local government organisations, which have frequently co-opted them. Kwa'ioloa is only one of many men who have been active in both types of organisation.

away immediately to look at in the Malaita Council office. They checked my work against the work of the Deputy Clerk and said it was all right. I'd made quite good sense of it, because I'd had a bit of experience of minuting meetings. It was my job as District Clerk and I knew about these things, so when they looked me over there was no problem. The administrative officers of the Malaita Council knew me and recommended me too, because day after day I'd come with money I'd collected for the rates and names entered on forms for the register, and the Council truck would take me around. That's how I became Area Committee Secretary for the whole of Kwara'ae, East and West. That's one of the jobs I've done during my life.

7 God's Work, and Backsliding

During the same period I was also elected as pastor for the Church of Mamulele, Gwa'ifata, Rabuta and Anobala, in the East Kwara'ae District Association of the South Sea Evangelical Church.[1] I was becoming more mature and God had blessed me and done good things for me, and that's why I was willing to do it. The election was between three of us and I took the majority, so I became pastor. While I was a pastor I knew my life was progressing and going up and up. At the time I thought I was just a boy, but when I held the pastor's job I was father to all the people. Everyone relied on me and if anything was reported to the church it had to pass through my hands. During that time I received many letters, official notes from government agencies and even from our leaders, Members of Parliament and leaders in the national church in Honiara. That broadened my mind and I learnt to do things which had been too difficult for me. When I spoke all the people obeyed me. It was a great thing in my life, because I was quite a junior man and I thought no-one would listen to me, but the true power of Jesus spoke to the people's hearts and they obeyed me. If I said 'We'll do such and such a thing,' we'd do it, whatever it was.

This also fulfilled tradition and I was happy to continue with the work, because in the past our tradition was for one man to speak and everyone to listen. If he said something like 'We'll make a great pudding,'[2] they'd offer sacrifices to a ghost and ask the ghost to bless them, and the man would make the

1 Within the District Association, each Local Church is a parish of several villages (in this case with headquarters at Mamulele), electing its own committee and pastor, who acts as a community leader.

2 In the past organising pudding-feasts (*siufa, sau 'a doe*) was a recognised way for a community leader to raise his name.

preparations leading to the day of the feast. Everything would go well and everyone would enjoy themselves. That's what I was doing. It made me feel happy, but it didn't make me say 'I'm their king'. No, they were kind to me and I depended on the senior men in the church. Because spiritual life isn't like material life. No, if I carried on and didn't watch out I could fall. So, with everyone praising me and honouring me and saying I was a good man, I got into a bit of trouble and started backsliding again. After two years I refused to do pastoral work because I thought 'Oh yes, I'm a good man and I've done my turn.' But no; as I worked for the Master, temptation came.

At the same time my wife became very unhappy about the work, because the more I did the Master's pastoral work the less time I spent at home. I had to visit each of the churches. Beginning on Monday, I'd sleep the night at Rabuta and in the morning on Tuesday go to Gwa'ifata and sleep the night there, and on Wednesday morning go to Mamulele and sleep there. That was my round tour and I was away from home all the time. On Friday I'd come back to stay with my family and on Sunday I went to conduct the church services. So because of this voluntary work for the church my wife was always cross with me. And sometimes when I was conducting a preaching band we'd go to preach in East Kwaio or go over to West Kwara'ae and run a programme there from 'Aoke to Kilusakwalo and Kilusakwalo to Laugwata, 'Afi'o, Fulisango and Anofalake, touring round all those places too.

It was while I was touring those districts for God's work of preaching the Gospel that I got high ideas about myself, and after I began my second year I gave up pastoral work. From that time Satan's work became more important and I was influenced by certain people, my wife was hostile to me for doing church work, and the more I visited around with the preaching bands, the more angry my wife was. We'd practise at Mamulele, which was difficult because we didn't all live in the same place, and I often had to cross the river in the evenings so we could gather there to practise our singing. Then when I came home late at night my wife wouldn't let me into the house. I'd come and knock on the door and call my wife's name until nearly dawn, I'd be hungry with nothing to eat, and I'd go back to the kitchen to sleep.[3] So the time came when I began to feel bad about it and think 'Oh, I don't want to do this work'. Because when I was a young man no woman could do this to me. I was free to sleep anywhere, to come back to the house or sleep by the river or whatever I chose. Now, when I looked back, it made me cry and I said 'Oh, I'd better change all this.'

Then one night when I arrived and she did this, I was really hungry and I prayed in the kitchen. I said 'Master, show your will to this woman. You're the true God I'm worshipping and I'm doing your work, so show yourself to her. I can't hit her, but you'll know what to do.' So God worked a miracle and my wife almost died in the house that very moment. Her belly ached with such an acute pain that she almost gave up the ghost. She quickly called out 'Michael, Michael' and woke up our firstborn son; 'Lawrence, open up for your father and let him in. I'm nearly dying.' So then he opened the door and I came in and said 'Look, that's my doing; God's doing. You've opposed him but the Bible says it's hard to kick against the pricks, and it's true. You don't kick against God; God's a man and he's our creator. The life you have was put in you by him and that life is in his hands. If he says 'give up the ghost', you'll die today, and if he says 'live' you'll live.' So that made

---

3 In most Kwara'ae Christian households (unlike Kwa'ioloa's home as a child) the kitchen building (*luma ni du 'urū*, Pijin *kisina*) is separate from the more secure and private sleeping and dwelling house (*luma*).

her repent and we both prayed, and when I prayed again for her she was healed at once; the pain stopped.

But she still didn't realise. When I went touring round again on the Master's work, visiting my local churches, she was angry and turned against me again, and then God showed her. This time she took a piece of beef which Sosoke gave us and baked it. While it was baking she went to the garden, but the Holy Spirit had already shown me during the night; 'Go home, something's going to happen.' So I left my work at Gwa'ifata and went round to the garden to meet my wife, as God's spirit had told me, and at the same time she left the house to dig up sweet potatoes. We met and I said 'Let's go back to the house.' She said 'Eh, you've just been chatting with the girls.' She was hostile to me again; Satan had got into her. When I asked her to go home we argued and eventually we both went back. When we were within twenty-five yards of our house, our house caught fire. The kitchen was burning, because she'd made an oven and a live coal from the fire she'd made was left by the sago-leaf wall and when she went it flared up. So then we both ran and everyone who was there for the butchering of the cow came running; 'Oh, the pastor's house is burning.' Pagan Le'a, my brother-in-law, and my sister were there at the time and they came too. So as we went I asked God, 'Oh God, you know I'm doing your work. If you're the true God, save my house.'

I went inside the house and my father said 'Go and take out the back wall and get all your things and throw them outside. The fire in the kitchen is going to spread up to the big house.' So God showed us another miracle; he made the wind blow the flames of the fire away from my house. Then I got pagan Le'a and some other brothers and we laid poles against the sides of the posts and moved the kitchen away. It was surprising that even though the building was on fire the sago-leaf didn't fall down and burn all my things in the kitchen. It all stayed up there and even when the leaf had burnt it didn't fall down. What happened was, when we'd pushed the kitchen away, it collapsed well away from the oven where the beef was cooking and the axes and bushknives and bamboo water bottles were all safe and nothing got burnt. Everyone was surprised. That was because I was a pastor and God had chosen me for that work and was showing the people his power.

But as things continued, with my wife being like that to me, eventually I gave up. I was backsliding again. I ate betelnut and did all the things I'd rejected; I accepted shell money from large brideprices for girls and took part in wedding exchanges. I was angry; I ate betelnut,[4] changed my life and Satan got into me and told me that even if I lived without Christianity I'd still be happy. I had a bit of education and I knew how to earn myself some money. Satan got into me as a ghost which told me what to do.[5] I didn't have the visions of my mother as before, but temptations attacked me and to make myself happy I'd join with pop groups to make music. That was the kind of thing which got into me.

I'll say something about a marriage I attended between Kwaio and Kwara'ae, among the pagans, the non-Christian people. Le'akini, a daughter of Timi Ko'oliu, was getting married and they'd paid for her for a man from Kwaio living near Sinalāgu, in the bush. I joined in the wedding exchanges because I'm born of an 'Ere'ere girl; my mother Arana was born of Bakete, an 'Ere'ere man. And besides, my sister

4 Betelnut, as a mild narcotic, is regarded by fundamentalist churches such as the SSEC as un-Christian, like tobacco and alcohol.

5 Kwara'ae often identify Satan as a ghost (*akalo*), of a kind with the ghosts of their ancestors. Indeed, in old-fashioned Pijin, *saitana* is often used as an alternative for *defolo* ('devil') to mean *akalo*.

Sango'iburi, born of the same father and mother as myself, was married to the son of Timi Ko'oliu, whose daughter was getting married. So according to tradition they had to give me some of the shell money, and that gave me a good opportunity to join the wedding feast and enjoy it. True, I shouldn't have joined in because by then I'd already come to the church and become a Christian, but I've explained how I was backsliding. I wasn't going to service and eventually I joined in because I was no longer a Christian but a complete backslider, a godless man.[6]

They paid thirty red shell moneys for Le'akini, and it so happened they gave me a *bani'au*, so now I was involved in the marriage. What I had to do was get a pig to take to the man I'd received the shell money from. The Kwaio way is just the same as Kwara'ae, as I found out during this marriage, so we had to carry thirty pigs to give to the Kwaio, and they'd eat them. I had to buy a pig and take it to Kwaio and my brother-in-law Le'a, Timi Ko'oliu's son, said 'Oh, you can take an extra pig for distribution.' That meant I could sell it off. For each shell money we received we had to take along a pig, but we wouldn't eat it; the person whose shell money it was would eat it, not us. That's why we were doing something to help ourselves. When we got there we'd have to pay, or rather give a donation for the distribution; you give some shell money and they give you a piece of pork to eat.[7] That's what the man's side would do, but they'd eat our pigs, from the girl's side, because we'd received their shell money. That was one good thing about the Kwaio. When I'd bought my two pigs, I baked them and put some of the meat and bits like the heart

6 Kwa'ioloa describes himself here as *uikiti*, a Pijin word (from English 'wicked') which often implies neither pagan (*hiden*) nor Christian.

7 Kwa'ioloa uses the Kwara'ae names for these events; *alutoli* or 'distribution', *kwate'a* or 'donation'.

and kidneys and things into bamboos and said 'Don't eat this, because they're going to come and buy it.' And although Sinalāgu is a full day's walk, those Kwaio really know how to walk; they must have travelled all night because they arrived at dawn. They just came, paid for our bamboos of pork, bundled them up and carried them away. The women put them on their backs and went back to Kwaio. We took lots of shell money too; they paid with *gairabi, la 'usu 'u, fa 'afa 'a, bani 'au* and shell money like that.[8]

Then when we'd finished getting everything ready we set out. First Timi Ko'oliu instructed us; 'While we're travelling no-one is to talk, we'll just speak softly, in case we surprise anyone as we go.' There were more than thirty people, men and women, and they loaded up all the pigs and went. Timi Ko'oliu was the leader and as he went he chewed some betelnut which he'd spoken over to a ghost. He went in front and as we reached the Kwaio border and passed the Kwaibaita river I saw what was happening because I was the third man after him. As he went he'd spit out a spray of this betelnut; 'Eh, clear the way; if any ghosts are waiting for us or sorcery or anything like that, if anyone has left anything to injure your grandchildren, you clear it away.'[9] He was talking like that to his ghosts. Then when it looked as though it was about to rain, he did the same with the sky too; he said 'Oh clear away,' and then there was no rain either.

Eventually we reached the village. It was the first time I'd been there and it took a full day's walking. When I arrived I

8 These are recognised denominations of shell money, varying in length, number of strings and types of beads.

9 Malicious people may leave magical substances, associated with ghosts, on pathways to attack passers-by, and people are particularly nervous about this when travelling in foreign territory.

couldn't see a single Kwaio girl who was wearing clothes. They were all completely naked and we really were surprised, all us Kwara'ae. It looked awesome and we were frightened; not so much amusing but rather good, I think. Then we put down the pigs a short distance away in one place. All was quiet, because the Kwaio were going to march in, decorated with leaves from the forest. There would be maybe twenty or thirty men holding bushknives and sticks and all kinds of things, and they'd shout and do anything to give us a shock and frighten us. So then Timi Ko'oliu told us 'Okay then! You Kwara'ae strongmen, you musclemen, step forward, decorate yourselves in the forest, grab your bushknives and long clubs and short clubs and get ready. When they come to tackle you, when they come shouting and running at us, we'll tackle them like rugby players.'

When I saw it I was frightened because it looked as if they were going to kill each other. It was a big event, because Timi Ko'oliu and the others knew what was happening as he was married to a Kwaio woman, Siubata, and they were his in-laws. So they knew the Kwaio customs well and when he told them they all stepped forward at once. He said 'This magic of theirs called *sīsigi*;[10] watch out for it.' He was saying that each man should guard one of the girls and as the girls put down the cooked pigs the men would follow them. They had to be quick in case the Kwaio shouted and came out from the forest and this magic came and injured one of our girls. We wouldn't be able to hold her, she'd cry and scream and eventually she'd die. That's why Timi Ko'oliu told these men to be ready to attack, so the magic would fade away and its power would fail. And they wouldn't be attacking unaided;

10 The anthropologist David Akin explains that *sīsigi* ('splashy') is a type of Kwaio sorcery thought to cause contagious possession, which 'splashes' from one person to another and is said to affect women in particular (personal communication 1994).

Timi Ko'oliu made the ghosts act for them too. He said 'Eh, go ahead,' he bit a betelnut; 'Ah, ghost so-and-so, work through your grandchildren so they can act. There's no other ghost here to do it.'

So the time came for the women to come with their loads of pork and put them down, one pig to each of the piles of taro which they'd laid around the open space to the side of the village. The place they'd chosen was a wide area like a playing-field, with several long leaf-shelters on one side. A woman would come, put down her bundle and quickly the man would take everything out and put it on top of the heap of taro, the woman would grab her leaf mats and run into the leaf shelter. They went as fast as they could, not looking around but looking away. They didn't see when the Kwaio came in whooping; 'Hu hu hu, kukukuuiia, aaa!' Oh, it sounded awful, and if you'd heard it you'd be frightened too; 'Eh, they're going to kill us!' The men, all strangers, looked at our men so fiercely and shouted at us, and suddenly the Kwara'ae men jumped from the forest, they knocked those men down, the Kwaio men knocked down the Kwara'ae men, all knocking each other over and laying each other flat. What a sight! But they weren't angry, just playing around and joking. Even so, they all fell down, some were nearly crying and some of the girls were saying 'They're going to kill us all.' It's just the way things were done, although it was lucky Timi Ko'oliu had told them to fight back. Rocky Tisa was in the fight and so was my nephew Sia'i, a boy from Mamulele, because I'd paid them to help me carry the two pigs.

When the attack was over there were the donations, when you made a contribution and they'd give you a piece of pork. These were sales by four or five of us, but the Kwaio men looked after our pigs and cut them up ready to share out. Someone would pay with shell money and they'd keep your shell money. It wasn't like with Europeans, when you'd stand there with your pork and they'd have to give the money to you. No, this time the men of the man's side managed everything; 'Just wait till tomorrow and let it go for now. Everything will be ready for you tomorrow.' They wouldn't rob you, they were completely honest. They were buying the pork that I'd brought along and when we arrived at Nakinakimae they cut it in pieces so that we on the woman's side could buy and we wouldn't be without pork to eat. The people gave a *la 'usu 'u*, ten dollars, five dollars, but the money stayed with them. Then the next pig was so much for such an amount, and they'd make donations. They wouldn't know who it was for; everyone gave, and we cut pieces for them until it was all gone.

One unusual thing was an old woman there who stood among our pigs as they did the distribution, and they said she had magic. If you put some shell money over her arm she'd know your name, so they said. As we gave our shell money we were a bit sceptical; 'Eh, this woman doesn't know our names. Shall we buy a piece of pork?' Sia'i and Rocky Tisa were sceptical too, but I asked Le'a, Sango'iburi's husband, and he said 'This woman really knows. If she holds your shell money she knows your name. She'll divine all the details, it's quite true. Listen while they share things for the people who've paid.' We listened and she called out Rocky's name; 'Rocky Sugumanu Kwala'ae.' He ran over to get his pork. 'Sia'i of Kwala'ae.' Well, we were a bit frightened. She'd tell a man's name and they'd shout it out, but with Kwaio pronunciation; 'Kwa'ioloa Kwala'ae'. We took pieces of pork and Fane and the other women put them in bamboos to cook and we ate it. They'd also made a big stone oven of taro for us, 'awaiting' as we say, in preparation for our arrival. But it was dry, with no pork, and we ate it with the pork we'd bought.

Something else also happened at that time. There was a sack of betelnut with the man's side and a sack of betelnut with the woman's side, and the betel-leaf was amazing. It looked like they'd taken a vine which had climbed a whole tree and coiled it up like a bush. And there was local tobacco like huge coiled ropes, two of them as well. We made an exchange, the betelnut and tobacco from the man's side went to the woman's side, and that from the woman's side to the man's. They laid out two leaf mats and each side emptied out its sack of betelnut, then the leaf to eat with it and bamboos of lime, and then the big ropes of local tobacco too. Then the men's side and the girl's side made an exchange, the Kwaio group ate everything we'd brought and we took everything they'd given us. It meant we were bound together by the marriage.

Then during the night they sang chants. My father Alasa'a sang, because our tradition is that when it's your girl getting married you have to sing the chants so that they'll do what's called 'going in'.[11] That means they'll give you presents, and when a chant finishes they'll call out a name. Sometimes they'll call out someone from the man's side so he'll think he's going to receive something, but they'll give it to you, on the woman's side. It's a joke and the man knows they're making fun of him because the man's side can't whoop it up for themselves. They'll go 'E, u'u aiaa. Eh; this is for so-and-so! Take it; take this ten dollars!' But then they'll give it to someone on the woman's side. That's the way it's done. That night the chanting went on till midnight and we got lots of money, lots of tobacco and they gave us all kinds of plaited bags.

Then something else the Kwaio said that night was 'Are there any men here tonight who want to chat with the girls?' We call it courting, which means just sitting down and

---

11 Epic chants (*kana*) usually narrate the deeds of famous warrior ancestors. The derivation of the term 'going in' (*ru 'uru 'u*) is obscure.

chatting, where they can watch you. If you're a married man
you can't court, but some women and girls came asking us and
we would have liked to; they came to us to sit down and chat;
'How are you' and so on.[12] But none of us courted that night,
because we were afraid. But they knew Rocky Tisa was there
so when the chanting had finished, after two o'clock in the
morning, they told Rocky to play the guitar. 'Eh, the
Kwara'ae visitors should do both kinds of music,' something
for the young people as well as for the old ones. They brought
four guitars for us to play, and I'd been a back-up singer for
Rocky, so when we got hold of all the guitars it went ahead,
'tra-la-la', until daylight. We weren't playing around!

Well, when morning came something else happened; it was
time to give us all our shell money from the distribution of
pork the day before, and from the night. All those who'd
taken our girl went into the forest and brought back all sorts
of bamboo poles and tied the shell money and dollar notes
onto them, then they asked all of us from the girl's side to
gather in that place like a playing field. Then they all came
whooping, and it was a sight to see. It was beautiful,
frightening, awe-inspiring too, because you could see one or
two hundred lengths of red shell money coming along. One
woman might hold two or three bamboos with shell money on
each!

They all started to come over, and what a sight! Now they
knew who we were, and the man you'd brought a pig for
would be looking after your distribution and he'd deal with
you. There was a proper procedure, with someone looking
after each person's takings. They'd given small amounts of

12 This 'courting' (*gunu*) respects the strict Malaitan prohibition on any
sexual activity outside marriage. As David Akin explains, it is common at
feasts in Kwaio, but strictly forbidden to married or sexually experienced
men (personal communication 1994). The Kwaio women evidently did not
realise their Kwara'ae visitors were married.

shell money but the people who knew all about making up shell money had joined them together during the night, not re-stringing them but tying the pieces together until they were worth a six or seven string *bani 'au*. We all gathered together, everyone came, and they'd put the money on your head; what they put on you was yours and however much there was, you'd take it. That way I received three *bani 'au* for just one pig, a really high price, and cash in two dollar notes; you'd be surprised. When all that was over there were speeches from both sides and then they let us go home. As we went back, Timi Ko'oliu went first and did the same thing as before for the ghosts to clear the way, until we came safely into our own territory. Then everyone went their own way back to their villages. That's what I saw of the wedding feast.

When I was behaving like this I also went back to things like restitution payments which I thought were wrong. When any man made trouble with my sisters and I received restitution, I thought it wrong. I remember feeling guilty about my cousin Tako when a man took her and ran away with her. Tako was only a young girl and the man was married. So then I went to ask for restitution and he gave one hundred dollars, which it was good as far as everyone else was concerned, but I myself thought it was wrong. I felt guilty because according to Christianity you shouldn't accept restitution and these things stopped me from settling down.[13] But it was correct according to tradition and good to accept it, because that sister of mine was only a young girl and he took her. When I'd received it I had bad feelings and when I used the money I thought I'd be happy, but no, there was no

13 'Restitution' (*fa 'ābu 'a* or 'making tabu') involves a guilty party showing respect for the person they have wronged by treating them as tabu, usually by presenting shell money or cash. Men demand this when their womenfolk are seduced because this infringes their rights in her. The church argument is that accepting restitution means participating in the offence or sin.

happiness. My wife and children didn't want any part in it and they said 'You can go and spend it on beer and things for yourself, but not on food.' They wouldn't accept it.

When I used restitution money while I wasn't a Christian, I don't think it helped me. It was wrong, like stealing. In tradition I know that a pig a man steals, even when he eats it he doesn't get much happiness from it. He can't enjoy it because he has to look around first and eat quickly and that spoils the food he's eating, so it can't be any good. That's what I believe about stealing things to eat, or stealing money, and if I use money I've stolen, even if it's a thousand dollars, I wouldn't have satisfaction because the money belongs to someone else and comes from wrongdoing. Even for someone who isn't a Christian I think this is very true, because when he takes something that doesn't belong to him, he's guilty and even if he uses it, it's no good. Maybe when he buys materials for a house, bad luck will strike and it will burn accidentally in a fire. That's the result. And furthermore there's life; he'll miss out on life from Jesus. That's what troubled me, and I came back and repented.

While I was in that state I nearly died, because I already belonged to Jesus but I'd turned back. Then I thought about myself and came back to the Master. No-one forced me, but I knew that in that state I'd soon be dead. So I soon ran back and gave my life to Jesus again, with the President of the Kwai District Church Association on Ngongosila, and when I'd repented I came back to do the Master's work again. Because I was sick, I felt bad, without blessing, no money, truly lacking in everything. I came back to the Christian life because I knew that if I lived like a pagan I'd soon die. I believe my life was affected because I was angry with my wife, and that's why I was backsliding. I did it because I wanted to show my wife, but when I was backsliding I had a lot of trouble and everything went wrong, so I gave it up.

The thing that made me come back and accept Jesus again and straighten my life out was that while I was backsliding some stories were invented about me. At that time there was a girl, just a young girl, who they suspected I was friends with. My wife had gone back to her place to stay with her mother, because the two of us were quarrelling about some family problems between us. When she'd gone and I'd stayed, after three months a man asked for a girl from a place near my village at Anobala. The man was a pagan from Arakoko, on the other side near Rako in the West Kwara'ae bush, but he was asking for a Christian girl. When he came to ask, the girl's father told him 'Twenty red shell moneys and one thousand dollars.' The father was with the pagans too and he wanted the shell money so he forced the girl to marry. So they sent the news but the girl refused to marry into the pagans, because she'd have to keep traditional rules which she wasn't used to, and she'd be naked. She thought about it and it seemed hard to marry into the pagans, but because her father wanted very much to receive the shell money she had to marry. Then the news came; 'Oh, on Wednesday those people are coming with the red shell money to pay for you.' So that night the girl knew that on Thursday morning the people would arrive to pay for her, she thought hard during the night and she took all her clothes and ran away.

When she ran away she ran over to us at Gwa'irufa. Her brother was there so she ran away to live with him. The night she ran away they searched for her and suspected that one of my brothers had run away with her. So at dawn two men came to my house to ask me, holding knives; 'Eh, you know, one of your brothers must have run away with this girl of ours.' That's how they talked. So I said 'Eh, I don't know what you're talking about. I don't know anything about it.' They said 'No, you must have come with one of your brothers during the night and run away with her.' While they were talking a girl from the house where she'd run to came along; 'Eh, that girl you're talking about arrived at our house last night. She heard she was going to be married among the pagans, so she brought all her clothes, and now she's there.' So the two of them withdrew their anger from me and went to try and attack the girl, because they wanted to get the shell money, and the girl ran away to the toilet where it was tabu for them to go.[1] The girl's brother said 'If I find you I'll kill you with this knife.' So the girl hid in the bush for a whole week and the people searched for her to attack her, but they couldn't find her.

But the problem was, she was in the area where I was living, close to my village at Anobala. Gwa'irufa is only nearby and it was my mother Gwamanu, Jephet I'ana's wife,

[1] Even Christian men will avoid the defilement of entering a women's latrine area, while those following the traditional religion might be severely punished for it by the ghosts of their ancestors.

who was looking after the girl. During the night she slept in her house and during the day she was in their toilet area, and she'd bring food for her. So she was doing wrong, and that's why they suspected it was me who'd run away with her. The suspicions continued and one day as I was working in the garden a brother of mine arrived. He followed the river, went up into the bush and came out in my garden at Anobala, and beckoned me over to him. He was hiding, thinking they'd recognise him, and he told me 'Oh, the people who've lost their girl think you're the one who's run away with her. They discussed it and put the blame on you. They say it's not a brother of yours but you yourself who ran away with her and hid her.' They were watching me all the time, hiding around my house at night to see whether I'd come for the girl, but nothing happened for a whole week. I know their suspicions and the things they were planning for me were because I'd pulled out of the Master's work. God was letting trouble come upon me, that's what I believe.

Then one day me and a brother of mine, Idufera, were working in my garden, because a letter had arrived from my wife, brought by a student from Gwaunafau school. When I read it she was saying 'Husband, come on Thursday to bring me home, with our youngest child. I'm thinking of you and the other two.' So I was pleased to be going and I asked my brother Idufera, 'Let's both go to the garden to get this taro into the ground so I can leave without it going bad while I'm away.' While we were going on with this the girl was in the bush, hiding during the day. She was up above my garden, between me and Nelson Bero's garden, because from there she could look over the fence and see any of her brothers coming and then hide. So we had a surprise when the girl called into the garden, 'Hey, there's a lizard over there!' She was pointing to a tree in an area of thick forest. The lizard had eaten until morning and had stayed there, so she told us, we heard 'lizard' and we both went up.[2] But her two brothers were hiding and watching us, so the girl made a mistake in calling us. We went up, climbed for the lizard and brought it down, and said 'Eh, go back to the house.' But she said 'No, I'm afraid they might kill me.'

So then their suspicions were confirmed and they said 'Oh maybe Michael's hiding her at the garden.' In the evening the two of us left the garden and went to bathe in the A'arai river and then we went up home. After we'd gone we didn't know what was happening, but it was dark and the girl must have come back along the path to my mother Gwamanu to sleep in the house. When she was still near my garden her two brothers caught her and threw her to the ground and put a knife to her throat. One of them said 'Admit that Michael ran away with you. If you don't, you're dead.' The knife was at her throat and she wanted to live, so she said I'd run away with her. She couldn't speak, but she said 'Eu', meaning 'Yes'. Then they took her and put her on my bed. They took her to my house, pushed her inside, beat her and threw her into my room at Anobala.

So quite unaware, me and my brother finished bathing and when we came up we heard the unusual sound of lots of voices in the village. I turned to my brother and asked him to listen, and we heard them saying 'Where's Michael? Where's Michael? That's his wife there on his bed.' When they asked for me I turned and asked for a small axe from my brother; 'I've got the big axe, bring me the small one.' I hid it by putting it at my side under my belt and covered it with my shirt. Then I crawled up, telling my brother Idu 'You wait here.' As I crawled I planned how I'd fight. The two of them would be standing there and I'd quickly get between them;

2 Large lizards are caught and eaten as a valuable source of meat.

then I planned to pull both of them by the legs and sit down so that one would strike the other. I'd pull both their heads down at once and bend my own head down and one of them would carve up the other with his knife. That's what I planned, but when I suddenly jumped up and said 'Hey, here's Michael; what do you want?', the two of them gave up. They stepped back, stood apart and told me 'There's your wife. Now live with her, and tomorrow morning you'll pay for her with twenty ten-string shell moneys.'

Well, now I was in trouble! I said 'Eh, what are you doing to me?' 'Ah, don't lie, you hid the girl in the forest.' I said 'Honestly, I couldn't have done it. My wife's coming; I'm going to fetch her tomorrow.' 'No, you're not fetching the other woman now. You pay for this one. Because you've spoiled her for what we wanted, for the man who asked her to go to the pagans.' I said 'Oh, I know this girl of yours doesn't want to be married among the pagans, and that'll be the reason she went. But you were suspicious of her and now you're blaming it on me. You should be giving me restitution.'[3] With that they ran off, leaving me with the girl. The girl knew she had a bad name with everyone and, realising that, she wanted me to marry her. She said 'Oh Michael, I'm upset because they've ruined my good name. When the young men hear of me they'll say "Oh, a married man has already had his way with you."' No-one would want her.

As a result the girl took all my shirts and trousers and put them in my big bag, took all her own clothes and put them on top, and took hold of them. Then I brought along my father Jephet I'ana, I went 'ssh' to him and his sons, and me and my father and brothers sat down together and made plans all night. As we planned I said 'No, girl; leave my clothes and stay here. I'll go by myself; I'll go to the police to sort this

---

3 False accusations may require restitution for slander (*suradu 'a* or *ilifata 'a*).

out. Because if I stay here, tomorrow they'll kill me! That's how it is, they'll kill me. If I don't give them twenty red shell moneys, twenty ten-string shell moneys, they'll kill me!' They made plans for me and because I understood politics I knew exactly what they'd do for me next day. I was only one man and if I'd really done it none of my people would have helped me. They wouldn't even have given shell money to solve the problem. Because I knew my traditional culture I was safe, but otherwise I'd have been killed. So we discussed it all night and it got difficult because the girl didn't want to stay there. She said 'They might kill me.' Then I said 'If they do kill you, that's your people's business. I'm not one of you. If they kill you I'll be better off, because you're the cause of my problem. So that's why I'm saying no; you must stay here and I'll go and tell the police.' By that time it was almost dawn. I thought that about four or five o'clock they'd come to the house and call out to demand the shell money. So then my fathers said 'Oh, maybe you should take the girl and go with her to the police and your father in West Kwara'ae. If you stay here something's going to happen. I think two of us can stay and wait for them to come.' That's what my father Alasa'a said.

So then I left my three children and went. One of them was only little so he was miserable when I went, but although I was sorry for my children I had to leave them. Fortunately at the time my garden was ready to harvest so I didn't worry because they could eat from it after I'd gone. But my children were really sad that night and the little one cried as I left, so I was sad too. But the two of us had to leave the village because they were going to arrive soon, so me and the girl went off to 'Aoke. We were going via Lalibaola and when daylight came we were at Kaibia village near Lalibaola. So after I'd explained it to them, an aunt of mine there, Kafo's wife who was a mother to the girl too, cooked some food and we ate and then left straight away on the Thursday morning, going through the bush to West Kwara'ae for my fathers Folota, Auluta, Bau and Daununu. Not long after we'd left the man they'd requested the girl for arrived on his way to Faumamanu to go to market, because Thursday was market day. He and his brother came after us too, so it became even more dangerous. They told him 'Oh, Michael has gone off with the girl they requested for you. They're running away.' They said I was running away with her to take her for myself, so that stirred them up and they each grabbed a knife and chased after me to kill me. It was getting serious.

As they chased me I suddenly heard them call out my name; 'You wait there; we're going to kill you.' 'Eh, my word, someone's following us, chasing after us.' So I turned to the girl and said 'You take our bag and go into the bush and hide there. Hide and keep watch. If they kill me go back and tell them at Kaibia and get them to come. If I manage to kill them we'll get away.' At the same time I turned back to thinking of the ghosts I'd used in the past, and then with surprise I saw the image of my mother. That woman had come back again. My word, I thought I'd left her through the church but now she'd come back, because I was so worried. She looked like she was alive, and if anyone did anything to me she was going to help me. It must have been the same spirit appearing again for me to see. So then I turned round and grasped my sheath knife, pulled it out and stood with it, and when the two of them came and spoke to me I saw them as if they were just little ants. Then I turned to them and said 'Okay, if you want to do something, do it. Or else I'll kill you both right here.'

So they were embarrassed and frightened. One of them said 'Eh man, this girl, even if she marries I won't be receiving shell money for her. And even if you have done it, you're a cousin of mine. So I'm not worried, she's not my girl.' But I said 'It's you who've brought this trouble on me. Why are you pagan men asking for a church girl? You're mad. We church people don't want pagans. That's what caused your problems. The girl ran away from marriage not because she doesn't like you or because you're bad looking, but because she doesn't want to go to the pagans, where she'd have to keep all the hard pagan rules.' So with that they asked for a smoke and I got a tin of Spear tobacco and gave it to them, and I got some stick tobacco and paper for them. They laughed and shook hands with me and we stood there and asked the girl to come out, and we smoked and ate betelnut and went on together. We had a good time together until we reached the village where their father was, who'd asked for the girl, and then they hid us both from him in case he was angry. They took us along another path around the village and helped us escape.

My enemies were kind to me that time, because the spirit of my mother had come to me again as a personal experience, and she was with me again. It wasn't something I wanted, but she'd come back. Why? Because I'd opened my heart to her and I was without religion. Then what the Bible says came true; seven spirits returned with another seven spirits until it added up to fourteen evil spirits, and my life became worse than ever. That's how it was.

So we went to the village of my father Auluta in the West, and when we entered the house he said 'Eh, this isn't my daughter-in-law man! You've come with another girl. That's not Bizel Fane!' So I said 'Yes, there's been some trouble.' He said 'Where's my daughter-in-law?' 'Oh, she's at her village at Fulisango.' 'And what's happened to you?' I said 'I'm in trouble, and I didn't intend this trouble either, but I've come for you all to sort it out for me, because my father over there is too old to deal with it. I've come for you and Folota; you both speak strongly about things, so sort it out for me. I've brought this girl so we can get the police to take her back, in case they kill her and we have to go to court to settle the matter.'

But the girl's uncle was in the West too, at Rako, near Folota's place. So while we were settling things during the night and talking about it, Folota said 'Oh, we'll send a message down to her uncle to come and take her to his village and he can take her back to their village himself. And you, don't go back now but go to the police station and report everything, and bring your children here, and your father.' But I said 'No, I don't see anything wrong with what I've done so there's no reason why I should leave my home and come here. Because my father's there, my garden's there and all my things are there, my coconut plantation and my pig pen, and all my people are there. You're the ones who've come to live here, on our land in the West.' They gave me their support, and something was going on. It was God, and I started praying. It was the first time I'd prayed for a long while. As I prayed the Master helped me and I went to 'Aoke police station. I sorted it out with them and they told me 'If they do anything wrong we'll take action.' That was that.

Now I wasn't afraid to go back home, so I went back and saw my children and my father. But before I went I had to see another traditional chief, Osifera. The two of us went along to Ngwaetingi, another chief, and we went down to settle things. By the time we reached Anobala my wife had heard that I'd married a new girl and that night she couldn't sleep; she cried and she made her brother Maelosia bring her home. Very early in the morning they came through the bush with our smallest child and when I arrived at the village they were there too. She didn't say anything; she was kind and sympathetic. 'Oh, you're in trouble.' Then I told her 'See, you fought against my work for the Master and now look at the trouble that's come over our family. I didn't mean it to happen.' Then she said 'Oh, I'm sorry. From now on you'll

be the boss. Whatever you want to do, I won't oppose you.'
Maybe it was all God's way of enabling that woman to see and
understand my behaviour.

The two of us talked about it, but people still came to
shout at me, telling me to give shell money. There was one of
my uncles from Taba'akwaru, who belonged to the 'Ere'ere
clan. He was related to my mother through the clan, but with
all these suspicions he got angry with me, even though he was
one of my own and I was actually his nephew. What
happened was he got so angry that he lost his temper and
came to shout every day at my house at Anobala, telling me to
give them restitution or pay for the girl they suspected I'd
taken and using all sorts of bad language. I wanted to go to
court, but they all said 'If we did go to court you wouldn't give
us a penny, because you know the law.'[4] That's what they
believed. 'If we go to court you'll win. We want you to give
restitution. It's all right, our girl can come home because she's
safe now. She can come back and we won't do anything to
her.' They asked many times but I refused to give any shell
money because I hadn't done anything wrong, which was why
I wanted the court to look into it. At the same time one of my
brothers wanted to pay for the girl for me. Mark Li'iga
showed ten red shell moneys to me and my father, with five
hundred dollars, which he was going to pay for me because he
was angry that people kept on asking for it. He wanted me to
be polygamous.

I'll just say a bit about this first. In the past our tradition
was that a man could marry two women, but he couldn't do
it without help. He had to use a ghost to make them both
love each other and be willing to live with one man and love

---

4 It is widely suspected, with some reason, that educated people have the
best chance of winning a dispute in court, where it may be judged according
to legal rules rather than local knowledge of the circumstances of the case.

Kwa'ioloa and family at his house at Kobito Two in 1984, still under construction, with its leaf-thatched kitchen.

One of the trucks travelling the road from East Kwara'ae to 'Aoke. Talking to the driver is Adriel Rofate'e, a paramount chief involved in the Kwaio compensation payment (see page 151). (1991)

Kwaʻioloa and Fanenalua with some of their children in 1991, including their youngest, Ben Burt's namesake.

A panpipe dance, like those witnessed by Kwa'ioloa at the sacrificial festivals held by his relatives in 'Ere'ere. The dancers (including Christians in this case) carry hornbill batons and cordyline leaves, and wear nut-shell leg-rattles. (1979)

Kwa'ioloa as a Special Constable in the Solomon Islands police force. (1987)

him. They'd both live with him, eat with him and share him. So our tradition was that one man could marry twice, but men like this weren't very common; it was just the ones we call 'important men'. But even though they were important men, they were still doing wrong too and in my opinion they should only have married one woman. But it showed how influential and strong they were and how good they were at making gardens. Having one woman cost a man a lot in the past, and to make gardens, feed pigs and earn shell money to help both the families of two wives, to give shell money all the time to support their brothers when they married, that was a big job. That's why I'm saying it was really only the important men who could do it.

I thought hard about that; 'Eh, if I had two wives what would I do? Because I'm only a young lad and I haven't got money either.' It was hard to say how I felt, so I avoided it and although my father almost said 'Yes', I said 'No, no, no; not that. It's a simple matter for me to sort out and it will be all right even if I don't give any shell money. They can't kill me, those people, because they're my people too.' So I refused and this brother of mine said 'In that case take something like thirty dollars and give it just to stop this talk, just as restitution.' But they said I had to give restitution of five red shell moneys, because they said I'd taken their girl and spoiled her good name, so even if she didn't get married they'd receive shell money for her. But I refused to do it because I knew I wasn't in love with the girl.

So as a result Mark Li'iga took twenty dollars to go and defend me, and my brother-in-law Le'a added another twelve. He had several ten-string shell moneys in his bag and several hundred dollars, but I said 'No, do it the hard way. Don't give it to them, because if you do you'll be spending your money for nothing. I don't even want to give them ten cents.' But he said 'No, if you go on like that it'll cause a fight. They'll be angry and say you're disregarding them. We have to put something in.' I said 'Only twenty dollars brother, and no more than that.' So he took them twenty dollars but they wanted more; 'No, it's worth something like forty dollars.' So my brother-in-law Le'a gave another twelve dollars, and they gave them thirty two dollars. They tried for more, but then they said 'Oh well, the man's explanations are reasonable, so we're sorry we've caused him trouble for nothing.' They admitted this, accepted the money and divided it among themselves, and the matter was settled.

But for us Kwara'ae, quarrels like this can be very dangerous. Only a week later one of my uncles, Bareakalo from Taba'akwaru, went to accompany the family of Lokafo, another uncle of mine, to Kaibia village to talk about Lokafo's daughter who a man called Ta'angwane from Dari'ubu had made pregnant. When they got to Dari'ubu to talk about the matter, Lokafo's son killed 'Aukwai, a boy from Dari'ubu. He killed 'Au, carving him up with a knife, and he died at once. Ta'angwane had gone to the garden and hadn't yet come back. When he did arrive he saw his brother was dead and grabbed a gun, and as Bare was still in the village he chased after him. As he chased him, Bare climbed the wall of a pig pen and Ta'angwane shot him in the back, and the bullet came out through his belly. He fell down and crawled along the other side of the wall and Ta'angwane went to find him. Bare crawled up into a hollow under some hibiscus bushes and Ta'angwane searched until he saw him. He brought him back down, took a rock from the stream and bashed him on the head until he died. So they buried him, and that evening while I was working in my garden at Anobala with my wife, the gongs signalled that a man had been killed, and I heard it. A message rang out to say they'd killed Bare.

These traditional gongs of ours don't tell the name of the man, but they give signals by beats which proclaim that someone has died, and when we hear that we know. When they proclaim a man has been killed, we hear it and we know. When they want to say someone has destroyed a village and taken the people or their shell money and run away, they beat it and we know. When they want to proclaim that something is tabu, such as the pagans' tabu period before a festival, so that no woman or man will go past their place, we hear it and we know.[5] All these messages are passed on by the gong, and that's how we heard that they'd shot and killed my uncle Bareakalo. Then the police went to investigate it and now Ta'angwane is serving a life sentence at Rove, and that man Sio, Kafo's son who cut up the other man is also serving a life sentence at Rove, and both of them will be in prison until they die.[6] That's a true story of what happened in 1981.

Then I helped Mark Li'iga; I said 'Since you helped settle things for my family and we're living well, if there's anything you want me to do for you I'll do it.' He said 'I'm building a house for my son,' his son Sina, at Namosamalua. 'It's going to take me something like two months to build such a big house.' What could I say? Because when I remembered the dangerous and difficult time he'd helped me through, it was worth more than the months spent building the house. It was a high price to pay in the days I lost in gardening and caring for the children, but my wife agreed. She said 'Because your brother helped you out, even if it takes most of our time, don't worry, I'll deal with the gardening and children and

---

5 These wooden slit-gongs (*'o'a, dram* or 'drum' in Pijin) use standard rhythms to broadcast announcements and news. The 'pagan's tabu period' isolates their community to ensure ritual purity for the festival. Nowadays gongs usually signal church services.

6 Rove is the Solomon Islands central prison and police headquarters at Honiara. The two men were actually released in 1994 by order of the Governor-General of Solomon Islands.

everything. Just come back home in the evening and in the morning you can go to work again.' So then I worked hard for two months for Mark Li'iga, building his house. It was a big four-room building with a high raised floor and I worked until we'd finished it. My father helped me, my brother Maniramo helped me to sew the leaf thatch, Mark Li'iga and his family helped me too. We all worked on it, but I supervised because I knew about building. It was a really fine house, the best, with a high raised floor.

So that settled things in my family and it was then, as I've already said, that I gave my life to Jesus through the church President. From that time everyone in the district knew how I'd fallen away from the Master and what my wife had done wrong, and everyone was kind to me again. I went around and testified and clarified it all to everyone and everyone was pleased with me, and I came back as Secretary of the church again and stood firmly with the Master. From the end of 1981 onwards I've been doing the Master's work.

9 *Work and Economic Development*

I'll say some more about how I came back and accepted Jesus again after backsliding. When I first took Jesus as my saviour, I've already said how I went around testifying and formed a preaching band. As I went around with them again I really became reconciled and everyone knew about me; we were friends again and I renewed the connections I'd broken off with the leaders of the church. That was when they put me to work on some important jobs for the church. They were kind to me again and I found I wasn't fighting anyone and wasn't ashamed in front of anyone because I'd reconciled my life to following my Master. It was then I went back to Honiara again. I left my wife at home and went by myself to ask for work, and David Kausimae took me on. I worked in the Maromaro shop with the storekeepers as well as in their fuel station filling up the trucks. At the same time I was involved in God's work in the revival in Honiara. When I came back they saw me; 'Oh yes, Michael's here. Let's set him to work.' So when I'd given my testimony and cleared everything I went ahead to do the Master's work.

The company also operated in 'Aoke, and I hadn't been working very long when the branch manager at 'Aoke left the job. Obet, a man from Bogotu,[1] went off and ran away. At the time there was no-one else to look after the shop, so David Kausimae sent me back to 'Aoke to look after it; the Maasina Enterprises hardware store. Kausimae wasn't a brother of mine, he's a man from Kiu in 'Are'are,[2] but because I'd been

1 Bogotu is a district of Isabel island.

2 This business, named after the 1940s Maasina Rul movement, was set up by people from 'Are'are in South Malaita and Kausimae might have been expected to employ one of them.

working in his store at Maromaro and he saw me work well and handle things in the way that suited him, he picked me from all those working there and let me take the big job at 'Aoke. When I reached 'Aoke a boy called Kona went back to Honiara for a year's training and I looked after the hardware store. When I'd worked there for a month I brought my family to live in the house in 'Aoke and we all looked after the store.

While I was in 'Aoke I went on with the Master's work too. I was in demand because I'd taken my preaching band everywhere and when I'd passed through 'Aoke it made me well known. Once or twice I preached in 'Aoke church. I'd taken the preaching band back to Malaita several times while I was in Honiara and, having seen it, they grabbed me. So I helped them and it was then I became a leader of Christian Endeavour at 'Aoke. Christian Endeavour was an organisation for young boys and girls to get together for social activities, to play volleyball and things like that, or go on picnics, and at the same time to lead Christian lives and study the word of God. So the young people would grow up in it and understand all about the church and religious activities, get involved in them and help their elders. I played a big part in that organisation, and at the same time I also helped to take services. As you know, 'Aoke is a town, where the evening services are just like Sunday services elsewhere, but as I was used to preaching in public I was very pleased to work with them. I made friends with other church members who conducted meetings at each other's houses and I also formed a youth group at 'Aoke with a boy called Michael from Makira. It was a guitar group and they called it Michael Two, because he was Michael and I was Michael too. I still have a certificate to show that we won a contest at 'Aoke. He was the manager for John To'omani's Hardware Wholesale at 'Aoke and I was managing Maasina Enterprises, so everything was easy, including getting the instruments. My brothers-in-law played backing for us and we two were the singers for the group. That made me enjoy the Master's work at 'Aoke even more.

When my wife and I had stayed in 'Aoke for a while David Kausimae wanted me to go over to Honiara again, because the store at 'Aoke was breaking down. That was because all the money I'd earned there was being used to buy materials to build the two-storey building for the Maromaro shop, which is there now. It's a big building containing offices above and a supermarket and hardware store below, in place of the other hardware store. They called it Pacific Enterprises. Then the government auditors came to 'Aoke and audited the shop. When the two Europeans and I did the stocktaking and looked at the records and they audited everything, they said 'Oh, everything you've done is all right'. By then it was time for my holiday, so Kausimae paid me holiday pay and paid for the ship to take me back to Honiara.

But when I got to Honiara something came up. I heard that the government was allowing local builders to take on subcontracts instead of relying so much on foreigners. That was the year I came back to Honiara, in 1981. So I rented a house at Vura, which cost me fifty dollars a month, but now I was working with my brother John Maesatana and we both registered to run a company. I myself named it J. M. and Brothers Construction, meaning John Maesatana and Brothers. It was mostly building and I was the co-ordinator at that time, which meant I had to negotiate the contracts with private companies so that they'd recommend us to the government and get us a licence to do the job. That made me well known around town.

It was just my brothers working. They were builders, painters, plumbers; everything except electricians, who worked for the government. Our work was just building, and by brothers I mean we were all of the same clan, the clan of Tolinga and Fairū. When we set up this company of brothers and went into operation they worked well and very willingly and really knew how to work. We even built the two-storey buildings for the College of Higher Education, and four staff units. And we built a lot of houses, from 1981 up until 1986.

But as the work went on I could see it going wrong, and the job I was doing was very hard work too. Because I was doing it according to our tradition; 'Oh, I want to help our brothers'. So we all worked but when I took my brothers on it was in the way of our traditional lifestyle. Brothers respect brothers, but they're not afraid to tell you what they think to your face; it's just the way we are. Sometimes when I was absent from work my mates would just eat, sit down and talk, and the work wouldn't move. So as a result I was making a loss, because the payments they gave me went according to the progress of the work as I'd estimated it. I realised the work was starting to slacken off and there was some gossip going on. Some were saying to others, 'Eh, that man's doing well out of you. He's making big profits and you're getting nothing.' These were men who'd done this work before but who'd ripped off their workers and couldn't pay them all, so the workers had come over to me instead. Now they were trying to influence my workers and some of them were misbehaving.

They were mislaying tools as well. Maybe they didn't think of it as stealing, but they were acting in the manner of brothers in the tradition of the past. Someone would take away something like a plane costing ninety-six dollars one evening, and the next day when he came to work I'd ask him 'Where's that plane?' He'd say 'I put it down over there yesterday'. 'Where did you put it?' That's how I'd talk; 'Did you put it in your box, or did you send it to Malaita?' I'd speak strongly to him but he'd deny it and pay no attention to what I was saying and I'd just get angry. He'd say 'No, I don't know. I just put it down over there before we went off in the truck. Someone's taken it. It's gone.' I wouldn't go and report it to the police because it was our old ways, my tradition and that of my brothers. Then all the planes, the chisels, squares, the spirit levels, all those expensive things were lost and it cost me thousands of dollars. Shovels, spades, and picks were costing me even more. They even threw away the wheelbarrows I'd bought when I wasn't around, burst the tyres, damaged the nuts and bolts, and when I got back I'd see it, but that was that. But I knew, because I'm not a man from England or anywhere else; I'm a man of Malaita, and so are my brothers. I'd just come and tell them 'Oh yes, tomorrow you can just open your mouths and pour the water in when you need to carry it!' But even so, I'd throw away ninety dollars for another wheelbarrow and carry on. It was drinking up the money and my brothers and I knew I was making a big loss.

It was because I was concerned for them that we bought a truck. It cost me seven thousand eight hundred dollars. We put a security of two thousand five hundred dollars in the bank, the bank gave us a loan for the truck, and we repaid it within the period of just one year. Because at the time we were working on a project for the Foxwood timber company, building ten units and earning two thousand five hundred dollars for each house. We could take five thousand dollars in one month, so that helped us along and that's when we got the truck. The reason for getting the truck was because I felt sorry for my workers. You see, I wanted to help people, but the more I felt sorry for them and obtained these things, the more problems they caused me, and that put me off.

We had five on our staff when we started. I was our co-ordinator, John Maesatana himself was the manager, Hamuel Fa'akaisia was the building supervisor, Wilson Fabo was the driver and painting foreman, and Benjamin Ramo was the electrician. The five of us ran the business until Wilson Fako saw we weren't making enough money, so he went off to drive a taxi and left us to carry on. We kept up the company until 1986, when me and Hamuel were talking and I said 'Hamuel, go and work separately, because if you stay the building side is going to be too much for you.' So Hamuel left the job and went to work for Juli Hardware, for the man we got the College of Higher Education project from, Mr John Whitely, and a Fijian called Moses.

All this made me recall when I lived at home. Compared to Honiara money was difficult, but getting a daily living from local food was very easy. Things didn't cost money, we just made them ourselves, but money was difficult because there weren't any projects to earn cash. That's why we'd all gathered in Honiara. Looking back at my story, I told how once the river carried away all my clothes and all our dishes, and me and my wife didn't have any clothing. That was just after I'd left Honiara and gone back to settle at home. I had no clothes at all; there just weren't any. I cut up a bedsheet and wrapped it around my body and I wasn't able to go to church service or anywhere else because I didn't have any proper clothes. Even with the bedsheet, when I was in the house I'd just wear a towel and my wife would wash it and put it in the sun and as soon as it was dry she'd bring it for me to wear while I was at home. When I worked in the garden I wore nothing. I was really poor then and all I had was plenty of food and work. Eventually even the bedsheet rotted and almost wore out. When I think about that time I feel quite sorry for myself. I was a useless man and really poor. Maybe if I'd known Ben, I'd have written to him in England and he'd have sent me some trousers, but I hadn't met him yet.

Well, to continue, one night I had a dream, and from our tradition I believe a dream is something real. I dreamed I was driving a truck and wearing a fine suit of clothes, with boots, long trousers and a shirt, and I was wearing sun glasses and a watch on my wrist. That night as I dreamed and saw myself driving the truck, I stopped in front of a tall building that the men were working on, a new one under construction. Then I called all the men; 'Come down here.' They came down and I took bundles of money out of my bag. I held several thousand dollars in my hand, paid it to the employees and explained their jobs and how they were to do everything. I took out a plan of the building and pointed at it, told them to order all the materials, they built it, I shook hands with the European managers, and they gave me cheques to make withdrawals from the bank. Then I woke up and cried 'What's all this?' I thought I'd become rich overnight, but all I had was a ragged bedsheet over my body on the bed. I cried that night and woke my wife and told her. I was really in a bad way that time, and we prayed that God would help us fulfil my dream.

But my experience is that this kind of dream can be very real for us, and when I came back to Honiara and made a subcontract with the government, I bought a truck.[3] That was a really big thing when I compared it to the time in my life when I had nothing but a bedsheet. The time came when I bought that big truck, because I'd won the contract for the Training College straight after signing with the government to operate a subcontracting business. When we gained that project it was worth fifty-six thousand dollars. The government met the cost of materials and everything and we just provided the labour and tools. Then one day as I was driving my truck I drove up to the College of Higher

3 When Kwa'ioloa says 'I', he is actually speaking for the group of brothers. This characteristic Malaitan idiom should not obscure the fact that the business, like their land and family property, belongs to them collectively.

Education and down behind the students' dormitories to the
two-storey building I was working on. I just arrived and
looked at my workers up above and they looked at me, and
then the dream flashed back into my mind. I stopped there
and cried. I cried as I recalled the time I'd covered myself with
a piece of bedsheet and compared it with that moment when
I was driving that brand new vehicle from George Tong.[4] We
didn't buy it second hand; my brother Wilson Habo had
picked up a brand new key, pushed it in, and off we went. So
as it was three o'clock and pay time, I said to the men 'Eh,
everybody come down.' But first I cried up there as I reflected
on my life; before I had a bedsheet, but now I was rich. We
had a bit of money; six thousand dollars in my pocket. At the
time some of our workers were building a workshop at Aola
too, about fifty kilometres to the east of Honiara. So I'd
bought a truck, employed workers, and when everyone came
down to get their wages from me I knew what an important
thing a dream is in our traditional culture.[5]

When I dream something it must come true. Some of the
things I dream don't happen, but only small things when I'm
oversleeping sometimes, but not many things don't come true.
There's a lot of truth in our tradition; that's how my life has
been, having only a bedsheet before and now having lots of
money.[6] I had workers, I had a truck, I had tools, I was
renting a house at Vura for sixty dollars a month. So I

4 This is the Chinese company which supplied the truck.

5 Another interesting thing about this dream is that Kwa'ioloa's ambitions
focus not on spending or consuming the wealth he possesses for himself, but
rather on sharing it out among others as the boss of a building team. In this
he is behaving like the traditional important men he describes earlier.

6 By 'true', Kwa'ioloa means that a thing is effective and works, as well as
being real; the Kwara'ae concept of *mamana* (Oceanic *mana*) which is
commonly mistranslated as 'power' (see Burt 1994:54).

compared it with my previous life when I didn't have a good house, when I had no money, no trousers, no workers, and I knew that everything had changed and my life was improving and reaching a good standard of living. I'll compare even further back to when I was a small child, while other people were looking after me and we lived in a house of bamboo. Well, I was in a bad way then. There was just one pot and when it had been cooked in you couldn't scrub it with steel wool or anything, no way. It just stayed there and we cooked in it as it was. We cooked the greens in bamboos.[7] Today, I've got good saucepans in the house, a cupboard, a table, a house with an iron roof, and my whole life has changed. I compare it with long ago when I lived at home, when everything was difficult and we didn't even have a box of matches. When I took some bundles of sweet potatoes to market I'd save up until I could buy a single box of matches, costing me ten cents. But at the moment even if I'm not working there's several ten-dollar notes in my pocket.

I learned about economic development while I was District Clerk at Faumamanu, working among the people as rate collector, registrar for the census and court clerk. The first thing I saw happen was people getting hawker licences and selling two or three tins of fish. When I was little I'd see an old man called Danidoe carrying such things from village to village, and my father would buy them. Then later on they'd keep them in a house and I'd see stacks of goods in the house and say with surprise 'These people are really wealthy!' But more important was selling produce in the market. We'd also sell copra, and if we wanted to make a lot of money we'd feed pigs and sell them for shell money. Now, as in the past, you can feed two or three pigs and if you're lucky someone will

7 That is, leaf-vegetables were stuffed into green bamboos which were laid in the fire; a traditional method of cooking.

buy one for seventy or a hundred dollars. Then it was just twenty dollars and that was big money; a man would feel rich. Then the time came when they introduced co-operative societies and I was surprised; 'A big store's arrived'. But these things didn't function well because people didn't know how to run them. They'd find a man educated to Standard Two or Standard Four and say 'You run the store', but eventually the people would get nothing because he wouldn't replace the stock. But now everything is much better, because the road has reached the East, people have big stores, they own trucks, they sell petrol, they have a buying centre for copra, trochus shell,[8] cocoa, you name it. The people at home have been lucky, and that's how I've seen development get going.

In the past no roads reached us in East Kwara'ae. The roads only served 'Aoke, just going north and south, and it wasn't easy to get roads there either. They were struggling with it for a long time as well as trying hard to reach us in the east by cutting inland through our island of Malaita. I want to explain my thoughts about the road. I remember when I was little going to 'Aoke when I had a big boil which was making me ill and my father and mother carried me. I was very small and it was the first time I saw a cow, and when I saw it I was really frightened. That's something I still remember. Well, we travelled and slept the night in the bush before we got across to the other side. Going to 'Aoke was a big thing for us in the past, and before we went the elders would speak for us to give us good fortune, because the journey was so hard. It was many miles across Malaita, and the drums of kerosene, the sacks of rice and other heavy loads, the women had to just carry them across Malaita. That was really bad, but although they knew what roads were they

8 Exported as a source of mother-of-pearl.

thought trucks could only reach 'Aoke, the place with iron roofs.

And it was also difficult because of our people, especially Osifera, who beat up a man when they were clearing the road. This was the road they planned to go into the bush, a short safe route, not cutting into the hills but just going along the ridges where it was easy. The road was being cleared by my fathers, local people working not with machinery, just with axes and knives. They were going first so that when the bulldozers came along they'd follow that route. But this man Osifera, who lived at Fi'ika'o, was very angry. I asked him once 'What were you thinking that made you angry with the road?' He said 'It's because this road came in and dug up a place which was tabu. In the past if it had been dug up like that, shell money would have been forfeit to the ghosts. And besides, I was sorry for the land being dug up. I want this green island of forests which looks so beautiful to be left looking as pretty as it is now.' That was his aim. A road was something which belonged to the ghosts. And another reason was because if there was a road people from other islands could come in easily. He said 'When they want to reach the other side of the island they'll just grab a motorbike or a cow and ride over there, and they'll make trouble with the women here.'[9]

9 Osifera's objections to the road were long-standing, previously voiced by one of his fathers, Filo'isi, when the colonial government cleared a footpath through the area in the 1940s. Filo'isi was the last priest of the great shrine of Siale, where, until the 1930s, a broad path or 'road' used to be cleared when festivals were held there, as a special prerogative of the Siale ghosts. This was why the ghosts required restitution, but underlying both Filo'isi's and Osifera's objections was a desire to protect their traditional way of life from interference by government and Europeans in general (see Burt 1994: 158-160, 214).

So then, when they'd cleared the road to a place called Alunabasi this man Osifera walked up there holding a long club and went and hit the man who was the boss of the local group clearing the road, whose name was Murumuru. The man was my uncle and he was struck by one of my fathers, who was also his brother. He said 'Why are you leading this group over places belonging to the ghosts? My word, nothing like this happened in the past. You're ruining us all.' Then he struck this man Murumuru and they took him off to prison. Osifera, my father, was in prison. It was his way of life and that's why he was so angry, and that's how the road began.[10]

Then because he'd put a stop to it the government changed its plans, but although Osifera had done this himself he really suffered for it too. The effects of what he'd done really changed Osifera's mind. One time the wife of his son Sale, his daughter-in-law Siu, was pregnant and ready to give birth and she was having difficulties because it was her first time to have a child. It was night and they said 'Eh, we need to get medical help.' But Osifera said 'My word, there's no truck. It's a long way to go, we're in the middle of the bush, far inland. How are we going to do it?' Then they just made a stretcher, in the middle of the night, and carried her. It was a very long way. Imagine it; the woman was about to give birth to a child, in difficulties and nearly dying. It was a serious matter. I expect Osifera's sons almost swore at him or struck him. So Osifera said 'Ah, next time the road can come. I don't like this kind of thing, causing problems for me. My daughter-in-law will die, all the shell money I paid for her will be lost and my son won't have a wife. And later I'll have to throw away another bagful of shell money to pay for another girl.' All this made Osifera talk sense that time, and the things which had upset

10   This was in 1964, and Osifera was sentenced to six months' imprisonment (see Burt 1994:214).

him so much made him cry. I just laughed at my father. Then
they carried her to 'Afi'o where a truck came and took her to
'Aoke. But when she reached Kiluufi hospital near 'Aoke, do
you think the nurses were pleased with Osifera? They told
him off to his face; 'Ah, Osifera, how did you get here?' He
said 'Oh, we carried her from the bush, my sons.' All the
nurses really laughed. 'That'll show you. You stopped the
road from going into the bush. You're lucky this woman got
here. If not, she'd be dead.'

Osifera learned his lesson that time. Now he'd allow the
road, but it's too late because he spoiled it the first time. The
government changed its plans and, as I've said, the road began
at 'Aoke and went round to Dala and to Ferakui and cut across
to Tiuni. They called it the Tiuni road. It goes round for
about forty kilometres, which is a very long way, and it's
brought us good fortune in the East, but this man Osifera was
out of luck. And he suffered too, because when he wanted to
make a permanent building, the bags of cement and sheets of
iron, his sons had to carry them and pay extra for help
carrying them up from beside the Fiu river! Now Osifera tells
me that things are bad for him, but it's too late. The road
won't go there, it goes around to us in the East.[11]

What was new when the road reached there was that
everything became really easy. When men were working on
the road they earned big money and people brought their pigs
for them to buy. And when they brought their market
produce, their crops and vegetables, people soon bought them
and that was another easy way of earning money from the

11 The road takes a long diversion through the Fataleka language area to
the north and was extended from Tiuni in the central bush to 'Atori on the
East Kwara'ae coast in 1973. Despite their remoteness from the road, in
the mid 1980s Osifera's sons built a new village of modern timber houses
with iron roofs and glazed windows right in the middle of Kwara'ae, where
Osifera continued to live with them in his own traditional men's house.

men working on the road. Then it was very easy for some of those who'd earned a bit of money to save it up and get a loan from the bank. Before it would have been very difficult for any of us to buy a truck, as I know because I've bought one myself, and several thousand dollars was really difficult for us in the past. But if a man could make copra and sell cocoa and maybe sell some trochus shells and turmeric and things like that, it was easy for him to raise a third of the price, put it in the bank and get a loan for the truck. When their trucks were based at home, my word, they might go to 'Aoke twice a day, it was so easy, and they might take one hundred or almost two hundred dollars a day if they were lucky, which was something we could never have done before.

This caught the interest of all the people in the districts the road passed through and now all the villages which were scattered around have come down and they've built their houses at the side of the road. And now I see them making platforms at the side of the road with sago-leaf thatch on top and there they put some nice pineapples and bundles of greens and when the trucks come they stop and buy them. They watch, expecting money to come any time. They're just sitting in the house and all of a sudden a truck stops; 'Eh, who's are these greens?' 'They're mine.' 'How much are they?' 'Oh, fifty cents.' My word, if there's no kerosene for the evening, put out some greens and when they take them, that's a bottle of kerosene. That shows how we've improved in terms of development during my lifetime. Everything has changed completely from what it was before. In the past we didn't know what such things were all about because as you know, we lived in our own way. When development arrived with roads and things it made everything easier for us.

During that time ATASI began operating the sawmill at Gwarimudu in Kwai District.[12] ATASI was a very great help to people here, coming and employing people who'd never been employed before. So they earned money to improve the standard of living of our people in the East, and it was also very easy for us to get timber to build houses. Even if we couldn't afford first grade timber, we could buy second grade, which sometimes only cost us a few chickens which we took to the Europeans, or other things they needed such as food. That fitted in with our traditional culture too, that they'd help some old people and others and then they'd bring them a chicken, and we all followed these ways of ours. That's how we carried on. When the Europeans arrived they understood it and we helped one another. That also made me pleased to have ATASI stay in our community.

ATASI came through the proper channels and made arrangements with the Solomon Islands government to carry out its work, but I have serious doubts about how they deceived the SSEC. They came through the mission and said ATASI belonged to the SSEC, but even so I began to realise that the things it was doing weren't to do with the church but for the sake of the company itself. Because the SSEC is just a church organisation which doesn't have money and when ATASI helped it pay some bills or buy things for the church, later on it would charge for it. That's how it took over some houses used for SSEC accommodation and took over the *Liutasi*, a ship that took the evangelists around to preach. That's why I didn't believe the company belonged to the church, so I started to investigate it. When I found out I was

12   ATASI (Alliance Training Association of Solomon Islands) was a company founded by New Zealand Baptists in association with the South Sea Evangelical Church (SSEC) to promote economic development. The sawmill at Gwarimudu, on the road near 'Atori, was set up in 1977 and managed by New Zealanders who trained local men as sawmill operatives.

quite annoyed and said 'It's just come here to make money and it's deceiving the church.' It also took over the *Evangel* and now it's sold it to David Kausimae for several thousand dollars.[13] So that's why I said 'Maybe we should get this ATASI company out of Gwarimudu.' The Area Council thought the same when I advised them, because it was a serious thing which shouldn't have occurred.

And there were things which seemed wrong to my people, which they complained about, and that's what the Area Council dealt with. They said they didn't pay overtime, they forced them to work in the rain and they didn't buy them tools. They brought all these things to the Area Council and so I took them up. Then they said they were only paying one dollar thirty a day, that they didn't watch the time, they didn't transport them back home, and other things which weren't quite right. So we argued with them until now ATASI is no longer here. But even so, we thank ATASI very much for their great help to our area, and now it feels bad because with ATASI gone there's no more work for the people. The people who worked there are now unemployed and they don't have any money either. That's caused a bit of a problem too, but it's because the government said 'ATASI, you're finished.' They went back to working in Honiara, not in the Provinces but, as I've explained, ATASI was a big help to the people of my district.[14]

But as we look to the future, our tradition is still the first priority for us in East Kwara'ae, so people reserve their land

13 The *Evangel* is a ship named after the vessel which missionaries of the South Sea Evangelical Mission used to tour Malaita and the Solomons from the early years of this century.

14 The sawmill closed in 1985 as a result of various internal problems of the ATASI company itself, and amid bitter disputes with local people over land and timber rights as well as working conditions at the sawmill.

for gardening and not for development. They'll prevent a man from saying 'Eh, I want, say, fifty hectares of our land so I can plant it with coffee.' That's hard to do, because in Kwara'ae the produce of our land is what we live on. That's why I see them restricting land and not allowing development in the East. Instead we go to live in town and the Guadalcanal people let us use the land to develop ourselves, while we're more careful with our own land at home.[15] But as far as tradition is concerned, I'm pleased that my land there is safe. When the time comes that development prospects are good and there's a lot of money on offer, I might allow my land to be used, I don't know. But the lands of Tolinga, Fi'ika'o and Fairū, my land, I haven't made any plans for them yet, because I want them to remain for gardening.

15 Malaitans living on the outskirts of Honiara are largely responsible for the extensive deforestation now occurring inland from the town, as they supplement wage employment by overcultivating the land for subsistence crops (as Kwa'ioloa describes the early settlement at Kobito Two).

10 *Tradition Shows its Strength*

It seems to me that our tradition really is still strong, and it won't change, because it makes us keep the peace and be kind and friendly. That's why, when they tell us to give restitution and compensation, we have to give it. Restitution is something neither Christianity nor colonisation nor social change could put a stop to in Kwara'ae. It's essential that if there's any wrongdoing with a girl or a woman, restitution must be given. Even if a person is Christian his relatives will claim it. This has been important from the past to the present and it really reveals our true tradition in Kwara'ae.

That's what I found some time ago, when my brother made trouble with his sister-in-law and she got pregnant. He's a younger brother of mine; we're descended from two brothers. The girl he made pregnant was his wife's younger sister.[1] You know these young men, they can't control themselves as in the past, and the girl was living with him and going everywhere with him. It's the new customs we're adopting of living with girls in the same house, joking with them and all the things we didn't do in the past when a man's house was separate from a girl's house and we only met up at certain times; that's what's causing us problems nowadays.

When she got pregnant they found him out because the girl revealed his name, and from that time her relatives wanted to kill him. So he ran away and some Kwaio men hid him. It happened at Luga where my brother was living.[2] They pursued him, and once while they were looking for him they chased me too. Because it's our way that if anyone does

1 This offence was especially serious since in-laws are particularly tabu to one another because of the conflict such an affair causes within the family.

2 Luga is on Guadalcanal and the incidents in this story all took place in and around Honiara, while Kwa'ioloa was living at Kobito Two.

something they'll also look out for his brother to kill him or something. They chased my truck in a truck of theirs, racing after me until I stopped and spoke to them: 'Eh, I didn't tell that man to do that to your sister. Me and my father had already paid for his wife. That's his own crazy behaviour. You go and look for him and deal with it.' We went on arguing, but I was related to them too, so it was all right.

When I'd explained everything properly I said 'If you'll leave this man alone, I'll find him and keep him in my house, and you can all come and speak directly to him. Because it's not just a matter of a young girl. According to our tradition, if someone ran away with a young girl you could forget it and come to me, and instead of looking for them we'd just arrange to pay for her. All right; but he's already married so he'll have to come back to the house to hear what you have to say. Even if you swear at him, whatever you say you can tell him to his face.[3] There's no way we can defend him now because he's already married. All I'm telling you is, don't strike him, don't touch my house and don't attack him in my house. If you do that I won't allow you to come to settle it up.' So with that they said 'Okay, if you see your brother, keep him in the house and we'll come on Saturday.' With that agreed, I sent word to the Kwaio people to bring back my brother to stay with me for the night. I gave him advice and asked our other brothers to assist him if they tried to attack, by grabbing hold of his enemies.

Then at five o'clock the next morning, on Saturday at dawn, everyone came and called out to the man. We all knew what was happening so we kept him inside the house; 'You just stay there. Even if they swear at you, whatever they say,

3 Swearing at people, that is using offensive curses, can itself be enough to cause fighting and bloodshed, although Christians no longer have to fear that the ghosts of their ancestors will afflict them for being defiled by the obscene language used against them.

just stay there.' I went out, opening the door, 'Oh brothers, say whatever you want to say, just say it. We won't say a thing. Go ahead and speak and when you're satisfied we'll talk about it.' They spoke until the sun had risen and it was about seven o'clock, and I said 'That's enough now. Perhaps you ought to stop and I'll try to give you the five red shell moneys you want. I'll hang them all up.' So with that I took a short stick and fixed it on one of the beams of my kitchen, and that's where I hung up the shell moneys, five of them. Two came from me myself, then my sister Ivery Arana hung up one to help me, and my son, the son of my elder brother Fasti Lekafa'iramo, hung up one. That's the way we help each other out. Then I took another two, one of which my father helped me with. So we hung up five of them and as they took them they said 'That's the restitution.'

Although it was restitution that I gave, my father Peter Finia also gave another five red shell moneys from home for death compensation, because the girl had given birth to a child and died.[4]   They distinguished the two and went for compensation from my father at home, at Faumamanu Tolo. 'Oh, the woman's given birth and died. Your son made her pregnant and she died, so you'll have to pay for her life. Five red shell moneys.' So he paid. In fact our minimum for giving death compensation is ten red shell moneys, so it was quite good of these people to demand only five. But what did they do but come back again and say 'Michael, you'll have to give another five.' There was nothing I could say; tradition wouldn't let me say 'Not me, it's not for me to give it.' No, I'm an important member of my family and my tradition says I have to pity my brothers and defend them. It's the same as

---

4 Restitution (*fa'aābu'a*), acknowledging respect for a person by treating him as tabu to make up for an offence, is distinct from compensation given as repayment for injury or loss of life (*to'ato'a* in this case, for a death).

in the past; if someone kills my brother, strikes him and spills his blood, it spills on me. That means I have to defend him and if he dies, die with him. So I said 'Okay, that's all right.'

While all that was happening I couldn't eat or drink, because I was thinking they'd kill someone over it. I devoted all my energies to planning and working it out, talking to them without fear until I'd dealt with it. Then something similar happened, although this time it was rather different. This was when my younger brother Jim Kwa'i, born of my father's brother Ishmael Lema, killed a Kwaio man during a religious performance at Kobito. There was a death compensation payment of fifty-seven traditional shell moneys and two thousand dollars, the highest ever paid in my lifetime.

It was the 28th October 1990 and a religious band from Mamulele on Malaita had applied through the Honiara District Association of the SSEC to make a visitation around all the local churches in Honiara. Then we church leaders asked them to come and do a performance to entertain people at the church with Gospel songs. They were playing panpipe music from the past which they'd changed to religious songs, and they also danced as in the past, but they were using religious choruses.[5] We were well prepared for people to come and everyone went from one local church to another. Hundreds of people came to watch and at Kobito Two that evening, everyone came and I myself was the organiser. When they began the music we'd already given orders that people mustn't cause a disturbance or anything like that. People who came along from elsewhere should all stay in one place and when another group arrived they should stay in another place,

5   This was a recent innovation; previously most Malaitan churches, including the majority SSEC, discouraged panpipe music and dancing as 'heathen' practices associated with the traditional religion.

so if anything happened it would be easy for us to straighten things out. Those were always our orders.

But while the performance was going on, right in the middle of it, I saw a man arrive, a man called John Faeni from Kwaio. He was drunk. He just went to sit among the women, near the house of Ishmael Lema, whose son did the killing. Kalaroso, a man from North Malaita who was married to a sister of ours, came and spoke to him; 'Eh, get away from these people, because they've made an order.'   But he wouldn't listen and didn't want to obey. Then he got hold of the man, because he'd been drinking too; he just held the man and pushed him. 'Eh, get away from these people, otherwise someone will see you and get suspicious and you'll all fight.' So he pushed him away but he stayed and came back again. When he came back Phillip Laura, a long-serving policeman who'd retired and joined the Reserve as a Special Constable, went over, and I saw him go so I didn't do anything myself. I was recording the singing, standing behind the group of girls who'd lined up to sing while the men were dancing and playing the panpipes. He went there and said 'That's enough. Stop it,' and took him away. Then he ran back again: 'That's enough.' A man stopped him and then he gave a challenge and swore and said some bad things. Then his brother Faeni, who they killed, took off his shirt and beat his chest and said 'I don't care about anyone.' That's how he spoke, 'I don't care about anyone.' Then he started to swear at the women and men of Kobito and use bad language. I was over on the other side from them and that's what I saw. Then a big crowd surrounded them and all I could see was the crowd.

So what was going on in this man's mind, my younger brother Kwa'i? He has the same name as me, but he's Kwa'ilalamua, Lema's son. He explained when they found him and got it all out of him. He said he was holding a knife as he came, hearing the man say 'I don't care about anyone.

I don't even care if I get a life sentence.' That's how he was talking. Then Kwa'i got angry with him and took the knife, and he didn't go down the steps; he said he jumped from the veranda onto the clover and ran. I saw him, all red in a tracksuit. He'd taken his red shirt and wrapped it around his head, tied at the forehead. I saw him run like that to the other side by the church. They were all pulling at the man to throw him out and we were speaking over the band's amplifier, and I was saying 'All right, we're the Kwara'ae; you Kwaio take your man away, take him away now, so we can get on with things. Take him away. Let the police take him to Naha and settle him down. Then they can sort him out.' But suddenly the man stabbed him and he fell. 'That's done it!'

The two men involved later told us police themselves, at Naha, the police station where I was often on duty as a Special Constable. I heard how this man Kwa'ilalamua stabbed the man in the belly with a knife. He said he'd intended to hold the knife up to him, not to stab him, but another man pushed it into his belly and killed him. Then another man said that he himself had hit him on the head with a chainsaw he was holding, and struck it against the head of the other man who survived, Alec.

So when that happened all the men there were very worried, because we were there when they killed him, and we leaders held a meeting. They killed him on the Friday and on Saturday we called the Kwaio chiefs to come to meet under the church office building. We came, calling our chiefs and police and they brought the police of the Fadanga, and Jack and all their chiefs came.[6] We talked because we hadn't found those who'd done it. The Kwaio were saying all sorts of

6 The Fadanga is an organisation representing the mainly non-Christian people of East Kwaio, equivalent to the body of chiefs who try to deal with disputes in Kwara'ae (see Keesing 1992 for an account of their activities).

things; 'They'll come and kill all of you if you don't find out who it was and tell us.' So I told them 'That's all very well, but wait until we take it to the church. We'll pray to God to reveal straight away who's done it, or else everyone's going to suffer.' So we put our trust in God and prayed. We prayed and that night this man couldn't sleep until day, however much he tried. He went on shaking until he himself went to report it to the police station. He said 'It was us two who killed this man'. It was the prayers, and we believe it was God who revealed this man so quickly, making him confess it himself in case all the Kwaio got resentful and killed a woman or man. We believed in God and we prayed. The Kwaio Fadanga had said 'You pray. We must hear who it was, or there'll be trouble!'

We were thinking that if Sunday or Monday passed without anything happening, we'd give what we call in Kwara'ae *firita*. All of us in the village at Kobito would contribute some money and we'd give it to the Kwaio. This was so that children, women and men could go around and if the Kwaio men saw them they wouldn't kill anyone else. We'd be removing the fear of killing and defending ourselves from anyone who thought to harm us. That's what we were thinking, but because this man spoke out we didn't do it; we turned it into death-compensation instead. So we discussed it twice, how to keep the Kwaio quiet so they wouldn't do anything, then we spoke to our people. 'You must all be aware of this and be careful. Don't go along the paths in the evenings, except for the adult men. When you women go to the gardens, don't go alone, and children, don't go out alone.' I gave the warning; 'If anyone does this and something happens, it's down to you.' We protected them well. Then we told the police station that a Land Rover must call in frequently at the village and the police officers must patrol regularly. We did all that, arranged a time, and then called paramount chief Adriel Rofate'e and his chiefs in Malaita to come over.

Well, it was me and Silas Sangafanoa who approached the chiefs from Kwaio, because I was Secretary for Falafala 'i Kwara'ae,[7] and Sanga is Paramount Chief. We arranged for the Kwaio chiefs to come and discuss it, and when we were ready the MPs for East Kwaio and East Kwara'ae, John Fisango and Alfred Maetia, came and said they'd deal with it. They overlooked the fact that the chiefs do this, not politicians. They played their part in maintaining the peace and talking to the people so we'd contribute shell money from the various clans to help Ishmael Lema. It was John Kwalemanu, Alfred Maetia and me who gave the compensation. Adriel Rofate'e and all the chiefs who came from Malaita tried to do it but the Kwaio wouldn't accept it. They wanted something like one hundred shell moneys, so nothing happened and that was that. So eventually it was me who gave it, when they called me to represent Kwara'ae.

So when I came there were the two MPs, the chiefs from Kwaio Fadanga were there, and the messengers or policemen of the Fadanga. Then our sergeant Eddie Samo from Naha police station came to represent the police, and the police inspectors were there. This was at the Central Police Station, in the recreation hall of the barracks. Me and the sergeant hauled along this bag with the traditional shell money inside. First we had prayers and the Kwaio group spoke, then Alfred Maetia, and John Kwalemanu who kept the money, spoke on behalf of the Kwara'ae, and eventually I spoke. I said 'Oh,

7 Falafala 'i Kwara'ae, meaning 'Kwara'ae Traditional Culture', is a name used by the organisation of chiefs, mainly from East Kwara'ae, for whom Kwa'ioloa acts as honorary Secretary, dealing with community affairs according to traditional values. As his comments illustrate, such grass-roots organisations (including the Kwaio Fadanga) complement the official state political system represented here by the two Members of Parliament.

this is an important occasion, and we thank you because you're accepting what we're giving to end the enmity between us.' Before I gave it I explained to the Kwaio; 'Oh fathers, grandfathers and brothers, we Kwara'ae shouldn't be giving shell money like this, because we don't make shell money. *Bani'au* shell money only comes from you Kwaio, and the Langalanga make ten-strings, but we don't have shell money. We should have brought fifty-seven pigs and extra pigs worth two thousand dollars. That's our tradition. But you can see how we've struggled on till we've done it, and it's a big thing for us. I'm saying we should be giving you plots of taro, or fighting weapons; that was our money in the past.'[8] I explained it to them, until they said 'Oh, what you're saying is very true; there's nothing more we can ask for. What you've done shows you've gone to a lot of trouble.' I'd already explained to the Kwaio Fadanga messengers, 'I'm a police officer who's been upholding the law for eight years, and I know that in law if we were to take action you could all be in the cells for what you're demanding. If you demand and we don't give there'll be more fighting and killing. So I'm telling you that you should be peaceable and just take the money.' So they accepted it; 'Take it, let's take it!'

In my lifetime, since I was little, this was the highest amount we've ever given, and I'm not surprised it was so high, because it happened between people of different languages. Kwaio is different from Kwara'ae and when this thing occurred between the two language groups with different traditions they demanded what was due to their tradition, so we had to give it. If it had been us it would only have been ten red shell moneys. That's why I wasn't surprised; 'True enough, that's

8 Although Kwara'ae use both these types of shell money, as Kwa'ioloa implies they usually buy it in exchange for pigs and gardens of food rather than make it themselves.

the tradition of people who make money. It's very easy for them so that's why they demand such a large amount.'[9] This shows that as far as compensation is concerned, our tradition is strong today and no-one can say 'Oh, the church or colonialism has stopped it.' Of course, as individuals some people say 'Oh, I'm a mission man,' but when you look into it, it seems ignorant and people say 'Eh, he's breaking tradition,' and it's true. That's how this fifty-seven red shell moneys and two thousand dollars showed our tradition was still strong, even though the Holy Bible forbids Christians to take compensation.

But after this happened we had a shock when the court went ahead and gave the man a life sentence! Because the law doesn't care what money you've given, it's just a straightforward murder case. You pull a knife and stab a man and he dies; that's all the law's concerned with. It's not interested in the ten or twenty, or the hundred or a thousand red shell moneys you've given. But we of Falafala 'i Kwara'ae followed it up and told them we'd given it as required. Then what? Me and Rocky Tisa made plans with Frank Ete in the temporary office at the Museum where we were carrying out our project for a book on *The Tradition of Land in Kwara'ae.*[10] We sat down there and dealt with it. Because Ishmael Lema had come crying bitterly, crying until he almost lost his senses,

9 Ten red shell moneys is a church-approved sum, but of course the Kwaio Fadanga mainly represents non-Christians. Kwa'ioloa might also have pointed out that when people take sides in a dispute as language groups the danger of violence is much more serious than between small groups of relatives of the same language. This, and the Kwaio reputation as fighters, is why the MPs became involved in this case and why the Kwara'ae side agreed to negotiate such a large payment in the traditional way.

10 The support of the National Museum for this bilingual book project (Burt & Kwa'ioloa 1992) also gave Kwa'ioloa a temporary base where Kwara'ae living in Honiara could meet to discuss local issues of tradition.

because his son had got life and he'd die without seeing him again. His wife would die without seeing him; that's what 'life' means. So I said 'Okay, we'll prove that our Kwara'ae tradition of giving shell money is still strong,' and I rang Mr Radcliffe, one of the Public Solicitors. He'd lost with Kwa'i but we said 'You'll just be the spokesman, because you know all about it and Kwa'i was your client,' and he was willing to do it.

So we wrote a statement, what the Europeans call a 'memorandum of understanding' and we asked some of the people who'd given the shell money and been there at the time to certify in writing; 'Yes, I honestly saw it with my own eyes and held the shell money in my hand, and it's true that we gave fifty-seven red shell moneys and two thousand dollars on such and such a date.' They all wrote it; Sergeant Eddie Samo wrote from Naha, Rocky Hardy Tisa wrote representing the chiefs at Kwasibu, and I wrote from Honiara, representing the people here and throughout the country as a whole. To all this we attached a document which we'd told the Kwaio Fadanga that their paramount chief Folofo'u had to sign, as well as the leaders of the Fadanga, their MP and the father of the man who died. We sent it off and when it came back our MP Alfred Maetia signed against their MP, our paramount chief Adriel Rofate'e signed against paramount chief Folofo'u and Ishmael Lema, Jim Kwai's father, signed against the father of Faeni, who'd died.

Nelson Konabako took it from here to Rocky Tisa, who took an outboard motor canoe on to Kwaio and asked those people to sign. We wrote a private letter to make contact between the Kwaio Fadanga and we of Falafala 'i Kwara'ae, telling them 'We're very sorry, but you told us to play our part and we did so and gave the money. So all of you sign the statement of reconciliation which we've prepared to give to the court for a final decision so the Chief Justice will acquit him.' It simply meant that we'd upheld the law and all the Kwaio were sorry for Jim Kwa'i too and said 'We accept that Jim Kwa'i should be released from prison because they did what we told them and we're satisfied.' Besides, the dead man was an outlaw who'd made girls pregnant and wouldn't take responsibility for the children and all sorts of things. That's what eventually led to his death, because the priests in Kwaio had asked the ghosts to destroy him and when that little incident happened he died.

That's why when we went to the Public Solicitor he allowed us to appeal the case. They saw the statement I'd written for Jim Kwa'i to explain how the Kwara'ae had organised his compensation, and when it came to court we saw once again how effective our traditional culture was. Jim Kwa'i was released from his life sentence and now he's home with his family. Three lawyers heard the case and eventually they changed it from murder to self-defence, because of another statement we wrote with Kwa'i which showed that he was struggling for his life and the man was trying to bite his throat and kill him. That made it self-defence and the case was acquitted.[11]

---

11 This case illustrates the tension between the legal systems of Solomon Islands, with its Western notions of criminal law, and of local people like Malaitans, who tend to treat all offences as grievances and disputes between individuals and their relatives. Whatever the decision of a government court, restitution or compensation is often essential to resolve a dispute.

11 *Tradition and the Decline of the Ghosts*

I know that everything is changing, and it seems to me that our tradition has been changing for a long time now. That's something that worries me more than anything else in my story, because now I have children and I'm worried in case eventually they adopt a different culture and then scorn my tradition.

In my experience there are three kinds of people in Kwara'ae, Malaita and Solomon Islands as a whole. First there are the group whose parents were the first to adopt Western ways, who are now employed as doctors, MPs and government ministers, lawyers, missionaries, headmasters, managers, businessmen and so on. They depend solely on monetary income and although they can earn thousands of dollars and run trucks, rent out houses and own plots of land, they're still not satisfied. They're the people who consume the land so they can live a civilised life and have others admire them and work for them, and they go overseas and imitate other people's high standards of living. That's not the group of people we belong to.

The second group just depend on their fortnightly or monthly take-home pay to settle their accounts at the stores and pay for food from the market, water and electricity bills, and some fresh fish, meat and chickens, but can't afford to build expensive permanent houses. This middle group often don't succeed in their plans but stay as they are, earning a salary but also making small gardens to save money in the market. They're not worried about being rich but don't want to be in financial trouble. My family seem to be in this group.

The third group depend on fresh food from their gardens; yams, taro, sweet potatoes, fana, tapioca, bananas, pineapples, green vegetables, pawpaws, maize, watermelons. They just work every day in their gardens and also earn a few hundred dollars from selling garden produce in the market, and the pigs and chickens they raise. My family are this kind of people too, and if we finish working we'll return home to live in the way I did as a child.[1]

But the way of helping and supporting other families has changed, though not completely. Those of us in Honiara support the people at home. For example, when my brothers' houses were blown away by Cyclone Namu the Ministry asked people to pay a fee of fifty dollars for them to supply roofing iron, nails, ridging and wire, and this involved the relatives in Honiara, because it's us who work for money. So I paid fifty dollars to Malaita Province and my brother got the roofing iron for his house. This shows me that the system of mutual support still continues today. Yesterday, for example, my sisters-in-law went back from Honiara to Anofiu in East Kwara'ae and I bought a bag of rice and sent it to the family my father is living with, and I sent a drum of kerosene, sugar and bread. This kind of support continues and I don't try to reclaim these things because I know I'm supporting them. But when I go and stay with the family at home who I support, they'll dig a big sack of sweet potatoes and send back a bundle of greens, nut kernels and things like that with me. It goes both ways and while they support me, I support them.

Yet although this is the way the support goes, it only applies to some people nowadays. With men who are already rich, who have fine houses, cars and all these things, sometimes the more money they have the more selfish they become. And with many of those who've been brought up in town and lived there since they were small, support for others is a bit limited too. It's those of us with no money at all who

---

1 These paragraphs on the emerging class divisions in Solomon Islands society were written by Kwa'ioloa as a comment on the draft text of his story.

support other people the most nowadays, and those who know the way of life at home. But support like this doesn't amount to much nowadays, and it looks like it's going to change even more. And the feasting, when we'd feed just anyone, children, men and women, no longer happens nowadays. What's changed this is development, because a man won't throw away his money on a pig costing four hundred dollars just to feed us for nothing. That's what makes it difficult for us; we want to do it, but it's hard. Nowadays a pig's worth three or four hundred dollars, and the reason is that we don't live at home where we can feed pigs for nothing. But in the past a man could feed forty pigs, or fifty or sixty pigs! One man could feed them, and it was easy because apart from the clearing where their homes were, the whole area would be occupied by pigs.

In the past we held to our tradition and it was very real for us because most of us were pagans. In 'Ere'ere they're still pagan today, but in the past there were important men and important priests. Once I went up to the pagans and saw how they held a festival and a panpipe dance, and if you saw it you'd be impressed and a bit overawed. Just to describe it; the sun is beating down and everyone gathers together to hold a big feast with pork shared out for everybody and they're enjoying themselves and wearing traditional ornaments and really looking nice. The women wear plaited cane bands and the men put on shell-bead armbands, cane belts, pearlshell crescents and shell disks; they hold short clubs and long clubs, put combs in their hair and put nice-smelling leaves on their combs. It all looks really nice, this traditional costume. I don't see anyone doing this nowadays, unless someone like Ben persuades us to demonstrate our traditional culture.

But today I see the practice of worshipping ghosts is declining until it seems to be almost gone, and I can see how this is. It's partly to do with health, when people live in the bush, work in the gardens and come home, sometimes without bathing, because there's no streams in those places high in the hills. I can see how they look at the ways we've adopted and envy them; 'Eh, I'm living all dirty and the people down there are enjoying life.' That's one thing that makes people leave the old religion. Another thing is that you have to feed lots of pigs, because your life depends only on pigs. When a child is sick and near death a ghost will tell you 'Oh, offer me a pig, and then my great-grandchild will live.' So that's pig after pig all your life, and feeding forty or fifty pigs at once takes a lot of time in the garden. That doesn't suit the younger people today. It may be all right for the old people but for us it's hard, and it seems to me that it's not because we're lazy but because the environment and our land have changed. As I've already said, when I was little I saw my mother just make a small hole in the ground with the point of her bushknife and stick in a sweet potato vine, and you could dig up potatoes month after month. But not today. Even if you have a big farm, you dig and get nothing; and why? Because our environment has changed. Our land is going bad and we don't know what's causing it. That's one thing.

And there's another reason why worshipping the ghosts is declining. We're all human and it's easy to influence people. While you're going on with your old religion I'll come to you and say 'Eh man, why are you doing this? Where we live our wives can just give birth to children in the house! Our sisters, when they have their monthly periods, they're still in the house! But this way of ours when the women wait by themselves to give birth in a childbirth house a few yards away from the women's toilet; sometimes they die there! Why are you living like the old people of the past? Those old people's heads are full of rubbish, they're mad. Come with us.' So one young man after another they make their way towards a simpler life which can help their wives and their mothers and sisters to live in such a way that even during their periods or giving birth they can stay in the house.[2] That's another reason it's declining and nearly finished.

And another reason is that nowadays girls and women don't like to go naked. I've seen this myself, because my sister Sango'iburi didn't like it. When they were at home and the others were naked she'd be naked too, but when she came down to a Christian village or to market, to the store or to town, she was ashamed to be naked and she'd put on clothes. The women and young girls don't like that, so they persuade their brothers and fathers, 'Eh, let's join the church and worship God.' And I've seen another reason why people are leaving. It's because they don't uphold the ways of the religion well and mix things up; they're not holy enough.[3] Their tabus are not up to the standard required by the ghosts, so people just die. The more they attempt it, the more lives it costs them. They're killing themselves because they don't know how to use the formulae which the ghosts used in the past; they mix with their women, they go into church areas and they eat the same food the women are eating. When they go home they start to die one by one. The standards of the ghosts' religion are very high and when they adopt these ways they're making light of them and killing themselves. That also

2 These 'women's tabus' are intended to protect the ghosts, and the men who deal with them through prayer and sacrifice, from defilement by women's reproductive functions. The rules are enforced by the sickness and death which may result from the offended ghosts withdrawing their support and protection or losing their power when their dependants are defiled (see Burt 1994 Ch.3).

3 Keeping people 'holy' (as Kwara'ae translate the concept of tabu into English) is the purpose of the rules enforced by the ghosts, especially those about women's defilement mentioned above, which set people apart from things which might injure or degrade them in some way.

frightens people; 'Eh, the ghosts are killing us; let's join the church.'

Something else I want to comment on is the lack of kindness there. If a man gets angry and a ghost makes his belly that way, he'll just kill someone for no good reason. So people who love others with all their hearts can't worship the ghosts.[4] Because if a ghost fills you with anger and tells you to take up a club, you'll even kill your own wife or child. That's the ghost. Of course he can be kind too. A ghost is peculiar; he's good in some ways and bad in others, there are two sides to him, and that's another reason why the religion of the ghosts has declined. We of 'Ere'ere still hold on to it, but I can see that in maybe another ten years time it will be gone. There's no way it can continue because once everyone has gone to the church it's hard for them to go back again. I've seen people who have come to the church and gone back and just died. One of them was Nguta, who went back to being a priest and died because he wasn't really established, and everything went wrong. Those are all good reasons why ghost worshipping has gradually declined, and I'm sure that when the old people die it will end.

But although we've come to Christianity we still look after our fathers and relatives. That's why once when I heard that an aeroplane had flown over the 'Ere'ere area and caused the death of a child there, I wrote a letter to the SDA people. It was an SDA aeroplane from their hospital bringing a woman who'd given birth, and it flew from Ato'ifi over a sacrificial shrine. I wrote to tell them they were causing death among our people and they were breaking the tradition of the

4 Kwara'ae treat the belly as the seat of a person's emotions, not unlike the heart in European culture, and Kwa'ioloa is familiar with both expressions. The complaint that ghosts can cause uncontrollable and damaging behaviour reflects the fact that they have the personalities and temperaments of the living people they once were.

country. We may be degrading our tradition in various ways, but they were causing death. They understood and co-operated and we fixed it up according to tradition, giving something as an offering to the ghosts, so then they were all right. I wrote on behalf of the pagan priests, Timi Ko'oliu, Maerora and Mae'alia, and they replied saying 'Oh thank you, we'll settle it and make good,' so we were very pleased.[5] That showed our tradition was highly respected, even by churches and government. Why? Because they're all Solomon Islanders and if they tried to destroy it, it would be to their shame. We are fortunate to have our independence.

Yes, my father was a priest for the ghosts in the past, before I was born. That's how he knew all about worshipping ghosts and how ghosts could behave in ways to injure a person or make him better, because he'd been a priest. I proved that was true in 1978, while I was living at home. Me, my brother Maniramo and another brother Rex Di'au, my cousin Filiga Takangwane and Festus Fa'abasua, we all went to a sacrificial shrine of ours at Fiu.[6] We went for the whole day, to survey it, look at boundaries and things like that. It was so we could see all the ancient things to do with the ghosts, because we'd only heard about them and not seen them. The place had been killed off in the name of Jesus by the missionaries and we thought it had been finished. But my father wanted us to go to a place where there was the tooth of the white dog of A'arai, which in the past was a ghost which used to kill people.

5 Kwa'ioloa's letter to the Seventh Day Adventist hospital, in Kwaio just over the border from East Kwara'ae, has been twice published in Keesing's studies of Kwaio (1982: 237, 1992:233).

6 This place is near the coast of East Kwara'ae, not to be confused with the Fiu in West Kwara'ae which appears on maps of Malaita. Filiga Takangwane was the oldest son of Ramo'itolo, the priest of Latea.

It died long ago but its spirit remained and it used to grab people and they'd die, beside the A'arai river.

When we reached the place where they used to sacrifice to the ghosts, my father directed us to the red tooth of this wild white dog. He told us to dig a hole the full length of an arm and when we reached it we took out two skulls. They'd put the skulls of two women on top of it, to feminise it as we say. I won't mention their names, but they were two of my ancestors and they'd put them on top of it to sort of dilute it, so it would be feminised and not powerful.[7] First they'd cut a stone in half and hollowed out both sides, put the tooth in the hole and joined them both together. Then, before they put the skulls on top, they put it in a deep hole in the ground at the base of a very strong tree.

When we dug it up and took it out, what should happen but a heavy fall of rain; we weren't expecting rain. We were in a bad way. Then as we watched we saw a tall man who took one long stride, squatted down, and disappeared. We all saw him; he bent down and he was gone, we didn't know where. Then before long my father began to pray, to get rid of him. I was a pastor at the time and when we prayed we felt him go away and our situation and the place where we were felt better, with nothing to harm us. My father took out the tooth, held it and he could somehow feel the power it had. As he held it he prayed, calling the name of Jesus. Then everything was put back in the same place. I asked my father if I could take it to hang around my neck but he said 'No; that's something you don't play around with. Even if it didn't

---

7 The women's skulls were expected to neutralise the power of the ghost dog in the same way that living women would destroy the power of ghosts by being above them or the men who worship them; a process known as *fa'akinia*, 'make it female'. The women's names cannot be mentioned because knowledge of them demonstrates inherited rights to the shrine and its land, which was what Alasa'a was instructing his younger relatives in.

have power, you'd be harming yourself. It's there as a sign for you. If someone comes and argues with you and you say your belongings are here, where will you be? In a court case or something like that you can point it out straight away and they'll believe you; 'Oh, this place is yours; that's why you know all its secrets.' That's why my father wouldn't let me take it away.[8]

But all the pagans are dying out and in 'Ere'ere the last people to hold on to the pagan religion, worshipping idols, the ghosts of our ancestors, are starting to die off. My sister Sango'iburi married the son of a senior priest and so a female ghost wanted her to become her priest. I don't know the name of this ghost woman, but she came as a blessing. She was something they'd bundled up in a leaf mat which had been smoked over the fire for so many years that the mat was ruined with the dirt. It was kept in the room belonging to the priest, and the priesthood was held by Osimaeangisia, the wife of Maerora. There must be something inside the mat, but I don't know what it is.[9] It inspired Osimaeangisia and she told Sango'iburi 'You'll take over from me, because the ghost woman wants you.' Besides that she came in dreams and Sango'iburi would dream that the ghost came to talk to her and asked her to take the priesthood for her. She came and told me while I was with the church at Anobala; 'Eh, this ghost woman really wants me to take the priesthood for her, but I don't want to.' I said 'But that's something you've

8 Alasa'a was referring to the possibility of land disputes, in which others might claim inherited rights to control the land associated with the Fiu shrine; a very real problem in areas like East Kwara'ae, with the competition for land caused by population growth and the desire to earn cash.

9 The object in the leaf mat would have been a relic of the woman ancestor, perhaps a piece of bone or hair. Maerora is the priest of one of the 'Ere'ere clans.

brought about yourself. Whatever happens you'll have to face up to it and get on with it and if you disobey you've had it.' Then she said 'But I'm not able to, because women doing this mustn't eat Christian food, eat casually or eat ordinary coconuts and things like that. There are so many restrictions, I might make a mistake and die.'[10] But what should happen when she rejected all this but she started to bleed, and she went on bleeding. It was very serious. Sometimes I'd treat her with the homeopathic medicine I had in my house at Anobala. It helped her because I prayed over it, so she got a bit better, but when I left she died because there was no-one to help her. It was like a monthly period, but she'd given birth to a child and it kept on going and wouldn't stop. Sango'iburi died in 1982.[11]

The senior priest Timi Ko'oliu has also died, and his death was very unusual. One of my fathers from home told me the story of how he was killed by the ghosts. First of all it was his wife, who offered sacrifices to the woman ghost, and maybe this was caused by a ghost. She had either diarrhoea or bleeding, so she went to the toilet and she collapsed. Maybe the woman ghost struck her down, I don't know. She screamed out from the toilet and that must have been caused by a ghost because you know a priest can't go to a woman's toilet. If he was to go there it would defile him and he'd no longer be tabu. A ghost must have done something to make

10 The restrictions are to make the priest tabu or sacrosanct, especially to defilement by women, and it is interesting that, while acting as a priest, a woman also has to avoid the very things associated with her own femininity.

11 A gynaecological complaint is the kind of illness one might expect to be caused by a woman ghost, whose powers particularly concern women's tasks and capabilities. This includes female reproductive functions, which can act to quieten men and male ghosts, as in the case of the women's skulls mentioned above. Homeopathic medicine has long been provided by the South Sea Evangelical Church as a service to its congregations.

Timi Ko'oliu worry that his wife was going to die and he ran to the toilet even though it was extremely tabu. Even before reaching the toilet, at the women's house, he shouldn't have stepped over the bamboo fence which formed the barrier to the women's area downwards from the house; that was also tabu. But he stepped over it and went on to step over the boundary to the menstrual area, with everything which was so tabu to him on his back. He went on right to the women's latrine, took hold of his wife, revived her and got her to sit up, and they both came back into the clearing, inside the housing area. When he'd left his wife in the men's house, the one where anyone could go to eat and chat, he went up into his priest's house and the ghost struck him dead at that very time and place. He died; he couldn't survive because he'd already reached the women's toilet. That just proves that this system of tabu isn't a game or something we just guess at or imagine. It comes right from our ancestors long ago, twenty-five or thirty generations back, with everything else on this island. That's why we believe in it even today, and the ghost killed Timi Ko'oliu.

But when he died like that the way of invocation which only he knew, to invoke life for everyone, died with him. As we say, 'the grub died inside the palm-trunk'.[12] He didn't tell it to anyone. Because with us, if a man is a priest, before he dies he should tell this way of invocation to a man chosen by the ghost to take his place. The words are secret and no-one knows the way of invocation used by a leading man when he strikes the first sacrificial pig, the big one he takes along first.[13] He presents it on behalf of everyone and then he punches its body and invokes the ghost by speech. I myself would be

12 *Ganafu* grubs, which live in the trunks of dead sago and other palm trees, are a valuable wild food.

13 This refers to the first of many pigs sacrificed at a festival (*maoma*).

afraid to tell it and it's really a difficult thing to talk about.
Even thinking of it makes me nervous because it's something
very important and a deadly serious tabu. Because he didn't
tell that way of invocation to anyone, I can say for sure that a
very important ritual was lost at that time. It's unfortunate
and a very unlucky loss. None of his children has it because
no-one was fit to do it. It was hard for the ghosts to choose
any of the other priests because a ghost has to find a suitable
man of the highest standard of tabu and when he looked there
was no-one. Timi Ko'oliu was longing for the ghosts to choose
someone so that he could whisper everything into his ear, but
it was impossible because there was no-one suitable among my
people in 'Ere'ere. As a result, when he died it was tabu for
any other priests to come and see him; it would have been bad
luck and caused big problems with the ghosts. It was the men
from the church who buried Timi Ko'oliu. The way of
invocation went with him. The ghosts which the other priests
sacrifice to now are said to be only the children of those
ghosts. That's why when that man died it was tabu for the
priests to go and see him, because he wasn't one to play
around with. He was a very important priest to us, Timi
Ko'oliu, and he represented Siale as a whole.[14]

I can say for sure that in 'Ere'ere, my own district, they still
follow that religion today. And those people were also the real
warriors, who opposed the government and stuck to tradition.
If the government told them something they'd take no notice
and wouldn't care. In particular there was the warrior
Ngwaki, who punched our big government officer Mr Bell at

---

14 Timi Ko'oliu, who died in 1984, was the last senior priest for the
ancient shrine of Masu'u (Anomola), and Kwa'ioloa's priest in the sense
that he is descended from the ghosts of 'Ere'ere on his mother's side.
Ko'oliu also represented Siale, the ancient shrine of the Kwara'ae founding
ancestors, as the last priest to offer sacrifices to the major ghosts associated
with that shrine.

the tax house at Faumamanu. He assaulted the church men as well, this Ngwaki.[15] He was one of the warriors there, but it wasn't just him; there was also Moses Gwagwa'ufilu and the others.   The 'Ere'ere people are the last ones to ignore development, ignore the church and even ignore the rest of the community.   They don't care for any of these things, and as for Europeans, they hate the sight of them.   But one day I went up to see Timi Ko'oliu with Ben.   Timi Ko'oliu just saw me and was kind to Ben.   Ben stayed and slept in his house and it's as if Ben had some kind of magic; Timi Ko'oliu, a man who should have taken a spear and speared him, Ben put his arm round him and stood for a photograph.

It gave us an opportunity when Ben came, which made us very pleased.   The chiefs and other younger men like me, who are educated but still traditional in our hearts, we haven't forgotten everything but we look back over Ben Burt's work and see the things which are lost.   We've set our goal to re-establish our traditions and we intend to change the things which are damaging our tradition nowadays.   We won't oppose the government, we'll work with it and the government will support us with manpower and we'll do things for ourselves.   That's our idea; we don't want to lose these traditions, except for worshipping the ghosts.   There are about four priests in 'Ere'ere now, but most of their children have joined the church.   It looks as though they'll keep up the traditional religion in 'Ere'ere for another ten or fifteen years and then when the priests have died their sons and wives will all come down to the church.   That's why it's important for us

15 Ngwaki, a comrade of Kwa'ioloa's warrior grandfather Bakete, is famous in Kwara'ae for trying to kill District Officer William Bell in 1925, two years before Bell was actually killed by a warrior in Kwaio along the coast. He also persecuted the local Christians who were trying to evangelise the inland districts of Kwara'ae around that time (see Burt 1994:129,153,155 and Keesing & Corris 1980).

to establish our traditional culture, and we have to talk it over, form a committee with all our important men and persuade the old men to come and be recorded and put their words on paper to put it into something we can read. Then our children, who are brought up with an education, can study and they'll know about our way of life too, so that they'll be respectable and everyone will be kind to them. That's all I have to say.

References

AKIN, D. W. 1993 *Negotiating Culture in East Kwaio, Solomon Islands.* PhD Dissertation, University of Hawaii.

BURT, B. 1994 *Tradition and Christianity: The Colonial Transformation of a Solomon Islands Society.* Harwood Academic Publishers, New York.

BURT, B. & KWA'IOLOA, M. 1992 *Falafala ana Ano 'i Kwara'ae: The Tradition of Land in Kwara'ae.* Institute of Pacific Studies and Honiara Centre, University of the South Pacific, Suva.

CARRIER, J. G. 1992 Introduction to: Carrier, J. G. (ed.) *History and Tradition in Melanesian Anthropology.* University of California Press, Berkeley.

FIFI'I, J. & KEESING, R. M. 1989 *From Pig-Theft to Parliament: My Life Between Two Worlds.* Solomon Islands College of Higher Education & University of the South Pacific, Honiara.

JOLLY, M. & THOMAS, N. 1992 (eds.) The Politics of Tradition in the Pacific. *Oceania* Vol.62 No.4 (special issue)

KEESING, R. M. 1978 *Elota's Story: The Life and Times of a Solomon Islands Big Man.* University of Queensland Press, St Lucia.

KEESING, R. M. 1982 *Kwaio Religion: The Living and the Dead in a Solomon Island Society.* Columbia University Press, New York.

KEESING, R. M. 1992 *Custom and Confrontation: The Kwaio Struggle for Cultural Autonomy.* University of Chicago Press, Chicago & London.

KEESING, R. M. & CORRIS, P. 1980 *Lightning Meets the West Wind: The Malaita Massacre.* Oxford University Press, Melbourne.

KEESING, R. M. & JOLLY, M. 1992 Epilogue to Carrier, J. G. (ed.) *History and Tradition in Melanesian Anthropology.* University of California Press, Berkeley.

KEESING, R. M. & TONKINSON, R. 1982 (eds.) Reinventing Traditional Culture: The Politics of Kastom in Melanesia. *Mankind* Vol.13 No.4 (special issue)

OSIFELO, F. 1985 *Kanaka Boy: An Autobiography.* Institute of Pacific Studies, Suva.

SOMARE, M. 1975 *Sana: An Autobiography of Michael Somare.* Niugini Press, Port Moresby.

STRATHERN, A. 1979 *Ongka: A Self-Account by a New Guinea Big-Man.* Duckworth, London

ZOLEVEKE, G. 1980 *Zoleveke: A Man from Choiseul.* Institute of Pacific Studies, Suva.